LayoffShield

Proven Strategies to Avoid the Cut List
and BOOST YOUR SALARY

by
Christopher Henson

Bloomington, IN  Milton Keynes, UK

authorHOUSE®

AuthorHouse™
1663 Liberty Drive, Suite 200
Bloomington, IN 47403
www.authorhouse.com
Phone: 1-800-839-8640

AuthorHouse™ UK Ltd.
500 Avebury Boulevard
Central Milton Keynes, MK9 2BE
www.authorhouse.co.uk
Phone: 08001974150

First published by AuthorHouse 10/19/2006

ISBN: 1-4259-5148-1 (sc)

Printed in the United States of America
Bloomington, Indiana

This book is printed on acid-free paper.

Senior Editorial Consultant:
J. Michael Henson
Golden, CO.

Content Editorial Consultant:
Diane O'Connell
Rego Park, NY

Cover Art designed by the magnificent Vanessa Henson

Acknowledgements

For my son, Jacob, for without his belief in me, this book would not exist.

For my beautiful wife, Vanessa, the love and magic in her heart inspire me ever so deeply.

For my son, Casey, who shows me just how amazing life is.

For my Mom, Terri, who shows me the true beauty of nature.

For my Dad, Michael, who played a major role in getting this book ready for you, the reader.

For my great friends: Paytra, Adam and Aspen Hogue, for their unrelenting support and courage in the creation of this book.

For my Grandmother, Mrs. Elsie Smith Gross, who has believed in me throughout my life.

For my wonderful family and friends who came to the very first LayoffShield Seminar in show of support: Momma Cita, Murphy, Todd, Rio, Dave and Charlie DeMarco.

For you, the reader; for without you, this book would mean nothing.

Table of Contents

Forward

You are holding in your hands the single most powerful career enhancement tool ever created. Based on proven, time-tested principles, *Layoff Shield* will provide you with a vast array of layoff avoidance strategies that really do work. If you want more, you've got it! This book was also designed to move you from a go-nowhere job to a career filled with pride, joy and accomplishment. Come with me and I will show you how to convert your real talent into money and have a good time doing it. Speaking of time, wouldn't you agree that the time we have on this earth is extremely precious?

As working professionals, we spend a better part of this time on the job. This time at work should be greatly enjoyed, highly rewarding, and above all, fun! It is my conviction that everyone is capable of attaining this level of happiness through the work we perform for others. Also, it is my most sincere belief that no one — and I mean no one — should ever have to live with the fear of being laid-off from their job. It is my desire to share with you the guiding principles that lead me to conquer the fear of being laid-off and that ultimately launched my career further than I ever dreamed possible.

In the pages of this book are the tools you will use to build a very special and powerful type of Shield. This Shield lives and works within your self, generating a dynamic energy armor of real protection against the negative forces that threaten your professional well-being. This Shield also acts as a powerful electro-magnet, pulling toward you the goals which you most desire to attain in your professional life. For me, this means working with fun people, making an abundance of money and doing what I love to do the most. I have all of this without the constant fear of someone else being able to take it from me. I am here to tell you that this is possible no matter who you are or what your background is. The value I offer you is the unparalleled personal empowerment to command and protect your career. Isn't that worth the fifteen bucks it takes to buy this book? Go ahead, take this book up to the counter and make it your own. You will be glad you did.

CHAPTER ONE

Conquering the Unforgiving Kings

A silence descended upon the room. I experienced an instant change in my entire body. I felt my blood pulsating through the veins in my head. Fear gripped me and began to squeeze, like a boa constrictor draining the life from its prey. The Vice President of the telecommunications company for which I worked had announced the bad news in the company auditorium, as hundreds of us stared blankly in silence. It was real. I heard it, but could not believe it. A massive reduction in work force was now imminent in the company. No one knew who would be let go, just that "it" was coming. I was scared. What would happen next? How would I ever avoid this? It was the summer of 2001, at what would be the beginning of the largest technology recession in the history of the United States of America.

Rumors and gossip spread through the company like wildfire, devouring the confidence of every employee. All anyone could talk about was how bad things were. People took turns speculating who would be let go first. The once upbeat atmosphere of my workplace was now darkened by the shadow of uncertainty and fear. During the days following the announcement, I experienced physical changes in my body. It became increasingly difficult to perform my job. I can vividly recall the awful sensation of my hands shaking when I typed on the keyboard. Headaches squeezed the blood vessels in my brain while I stared at the computer screen. It took all I had to actually do the work.

The panic-stricken consciousness of my workplace continued to haunt me at home. Too anxious to sleep, I continuously focused on what it would be like if I lost my job. I spent many nights playing out different lay-off scenarios in my mind. How long before I am laid-off? How will I tell my wife when it happens? How long will the apartment leasing agency let us stay here before an eviction notice appears on the door? Where would we go if we did get evicted? Who can I ask for money? These thoughts looped endlessly in my mind. I was so scared, I could not think about anything else. The worry ruled my mind like an unforgiving King who abuses his power and all of his subjects.

One particular night, when my body was too exhausted to stay awake a second longer, I drifted off into a very life-like nightmare. It unfolded just like the beginning of another day, behind the wheel of my trusty Honda Prelude, driving to work. In the dream I arrived at work and pulled my car up to the main entrance gate of the parking garage. (The parking garage is secure and an access badge is required to lift the gate and gain entrance.) I rolled down my window, reached out with my access badge and swiped it across the black reader box. Instantly, a red light appeared on the reader box, accompanied by a loud electronic buzz. I swiped my badge one more time. The hindering red light appeared again and the reader buzzed once more, this time much louder.

A security guard had overheard the buzz and was quickly approaching me. Next, I found myself being escorted to the human resources office. I was frozen with fear.

The nightmare fast-forwarded in time with a sickening blur. I found myself getting back in my car with my box of belongings and my termination paperwork in hand. The single worst part of that dream was the awful feeling that had seized my body when I was contemplating how to tell my wife that I had been let go from my job. I felt sick inside. My stomach wrenched inside me as I slept. Even after I awoke the next morning, that horrible feeling did not leave me for several hours.

Looking back with full hindsight, my company had not yet let me go, but it seemed my *mind* was the one who had placed me on the cut-list and laid me off. I did my best to hide the fear from my family. However, fear is a difficult thing to keep bottled up inside because the pressure continues to build and the emotions become too powerful to contain. When fear that has been bottled up for a long time does, in fact, escape, it comes out as something other than fear.

One evening, not too long after the pending layoff announcement, my three-year-old son, Jake, wanted to tell me about the painting he'd made that day. At that moment, however, my attention was completely absorbed by my computer. Jake tugged on my sleeve and his little voice piped, "Dad! Dad! Dad! Dad! Dad!" I snapped. I burst at him with an intense anger in my voice, "WHAT JAKE!? WHAT DO YOU WANT?!!" This, of course, immediately caused him to burst into tears. I felt terrible. Intense guilt saturated my mind after I realized I had scolded him for absolutely no reason. It was my job to take care of Jake, and somehow, I felt I had just failed him. I felt like I had lost complete control. My thoughts cascaded downhill. I wondered how I would take care of him if I were let go from my job. What kind of Dad would I be? It was the worst feeling in the world.

After having just witnessed this unwarranted explosion of anger, my wife, Vanessa, knew right then and there that something was not right with me. I could hide my fear no longer. When Vanessa asked me what was really wrong, I was hesitant to tell her, simply because I so wanted to protect her. She was not going to let me go until she got the truth. She deserved the truth. I told her everything. As I spoke, the expression on my face told her more about how worried I really was than the words that came out of my mouth. Tears welled up in her eyes as the worry and fear made its way from me into her. Vanessa started sobbing. I grabbed her and held her in my arms while she cried.

The First Fragments of Steel

Next, something very unexpected happened. In that moment, feeling my wife cry changed something inside of me. Inside the black void of guilt, sadness and fear, a new thought was instantly born. *I will not let myself be laid-off!* This new thought would be the spark that would ignite an unstoppable force! Another powerful thought followed right on the heels of the first one. *My company does not decide my destiny. I do!* This realization immediately annihilated all the negative visions that ruled the land inside my head. These two thoughts were the first fragments of steel from which I forged my own *LayoffShield*. Both thoughts were fueled by an intense desire to protect my family from poverty, fear and all of the forces that had been threatening us.

That night, I lay wide awake in bed with my eyes fixed firmly on the ceiling above me, pondering the two new thoughts that had come into my mind. For the first time since the company announcement, my main focus was not on the fear of being let go from my job, but on something entirely different. A new determination was now living and breathing inside me. At that particular moment in time, I had absolutely no idea how I was going to avoid what seemed to be unavoidable. All I had was a new definite purpose, a force pushing at me from the inside.

The next morning, I began the day with a brand new kind of thinking, the kind of thinking that did not include worry and fear. My mission was now clear. Somehow, I had to turn the tides in my favor. I needed to know how and I needed to know it quickly. I needed the proper components to build some kind of plan.

The Quest Begins

I had to act fast. The entire US economy seemed to be against me, especially in my own field, the telecommunications sector. New jobs were said to be "impossible" to find. Most of the people at my work clung tightly to their flailing employment, not even attempting to look elsewhere because the media had painted such a bleak picture of the economy. Every day there were headlines about mass layoffs happening somewhere. An imposing shadow had been cast over the land. I was standing in the middle of it, looking for the tiniest ray of light.

At that time, there were no books available on how to protect oneself from being laid-off. Nothing! But it didn't matter. I knew the answers I was looking for were out there somewhere. They just had to be. I started searching for books and information on people who had been faced with incredible odds, and who were able triumph, regardless of circumstances that stood against them. It became my passion, my mission, to find every possible method of surmounting difficultly and to put those methods into immediate use. I spent hours listening to audio books, reading stacks of biographies and even attended seminars to find the answers I needed. During every spare moment of time, I was seeking and learning. I studied many different success philosophies, biographies and ideas, pulling from each of them anything that would help me protect my job.

I took action immediately to protect my employment. Over time, the specialized knowledge I had acquired, combined with uninhibited action, allowed me to avoid what millions of others could not. This was the massive layoff tidal wave that swept over the American economy, beginning in 2001. This tidal wave took millions of jobs with it. The US Bureau of Labor Statistics recorded 2,495,937 layoffs in the year 2001. Another 1,976,291 people had their employment involuntarily terminated in 2002. That totals four and a half million people who lost their jobs in just two years, people who had families and children.

In the beginning, all I wanted was to figure out how to dodge the cut-list. However, through my research, and by using what I had learned, I discovered something far more valuable. Using the same specialized knowledge that had saved me, I was able to move ahead. During this major recession, I moved onto new jobs, boosting my income significantly each time. In fact, I changed jobs three times in three years, on my own terms, beating out hundreds of other job candidates with every move! I don't say this to impress you. I say it simply to relay how powerful the information in this book is, and that it really does work!

You've Got It!

Now this same knowledge belongs to you. It comes to you in the form of a Shield designed to protect you. A *LayoffShield.* Why a shield? The shield has been a most effective defensive weapon throughout history. The very nature of a shield is its ability to stop a direct attack from an enemy, leaving its holder unscathed and untouched. The shields that belonged to the Knights of King Arthur were forged from tempered steel, and the Knights depended on the strength of their shields to guard their lives in the most brutal of battles. Roman Gladiators also depended heavily upon the shield to deflect deadly attacks when battling for their lives in the Grand Coliseum.

Centuries upon centuries have passed, and yet a shield is still necessary to protect those who venture out daily to do battle. This is the *LayoffShield* . This modern day shield is designed to protect you from any force that would threaten your job, threaten your career or threaten the flow of money into your life. The same knowledge used to protect yourself can also be used to create opportunities for you, allowing for major advancement in the professional arenas. This is exactly what occurred in my career when I began putting what I had learned into action. Today,

I work with great people at a job I love, earning a salary higher than I'd ever dreamed and without the constant fear of having the rug pulled out from under me.

This level of professional security, job satisfaction and healthy income is something that I strongly believe must be shared, and that everyone does, in fact, deserve such riches. Even more important, I know these goals are possible to attain no matter who you are or what your level of education may be. The *LayoffShield* is inherently powerful, and it will work for you the way it has for me. That is a promise.

What Does the *LayoffShield* Do?

Your *LayoffShield* arms you with three powerful forces, which allow you to:

1) Avoid a cut-list completely and excel to great heights with your current employer.
2) Secure new and stable employment before a layoff threat can affect you, without gaps in your continuous income.
3) Work a master plan of your personal design to obtain financial freedom through your talent, performing the kind of work you want to be doing.

You may choose to forge your *LayoffShield* to one or all of the strengths listed above, customizing your Shield to fit your grasp and purpose. However you use it, the *LayoffShield* will empower you to take complete control of your professional life. Born from hundreds of hours of intense research and practical life application, this book is designed to impart maximum benefit to you, regardless of your profession. As you turn the pages of this book and are absorbing its contents, keep in mind this important truth: You possess the capability to influence your career to a degree far greater than you have previously dreamed possible.

> *"Readiness is all."*
> **-William Shakespeare**

CHAPTER TWO

Taking Control of Your Destiny

The first significant advancement I made toward constructing an effective *LayoffShield* was based on the idea of moving away from fear. I was so panicked when I found out I could be laid-off. The first step was to once and for all rid myself of that fear. How? Through my research and studies of men and women whom I considered great, I discovered that all those who had conquered seemingly insurmountable odds had one major thing in common: they all refused to compromise with unwanted circumstances. Simply put, they did not submit to the forces that attempted to take control of their lives.

The great men and women I have studied all embraced their own individual capacity to control and manipulate their own minds to create the circumstances they truly desired inside themselves *first*, before ever taking any outside action. They drew from an environment that was completely under their control when the outside world was fully against them; allowing them consistently to deal from a position of strength. Another defining characteristic of these great people was that they all recognized their own limitless potential; and by sticking to that conviction in the midst of adversity, the once impossible challenges that blocked their path became scattered pieces of armor on the battlefield.

Here is a quick glimpse at some of the amazing people whose actions became the framework of the first *LayoffShield*.

One of the most profound illustrations of an individual who did not submit to the forces that attempted to take control of his career is President Franklin D. Roosevelt. It is a well known fact that in 1921, Roosevelt contracted a severe case of polio, which robbed him of the use of his legs and sentenced him to life in a wheelchair. What the history books often neglect to mention was the immense power that was in Roosevelt's mind. Rather than allowing the disease to destroy his confidence and ruin his career, Roosevelt focused his thoughts on self-reliance and concentrated on his professional abilities as a politician. He did this so well, that he was able to sell himself successfully to the public and win the Governor's seat of New York in 1928. This feat was just the beginning. The incredible mastery Roosevelt enacted over his mind continued to elevate his career over the next fifteen years, permitting him to win *four* Presidential terms and become one of the most famous and well respected Presidents in US history. What Roosevelt did was nothing less than incredible!

Another equally powerful example of a person who refused to compromise with unwanted circumstances is Rosa Parks. Although Rosa Parks' experience was not tied to her career per-se, I mention her here because she is one of the finest examples of an individual who would not allow outside forces to determine her destiny, which is the very idea behind the *LayoffShield*. You may already know Rosa Parks' amazing story, but for those who don't, here is a brief account.

In 1955, in Montgomery, Alabama, while riding home on a city bus, Rosa Parks refused to relinquish her seat to a person of "non-color" when the bus driver demanded she stand up and move. When Parks did not acquiesce, the bus driver became angry, threatening her with civil disobedience charges. It did not matter. Rosa Parks still did not budge. As a result, she was arrested for her refusal to obey. As the news of her story cascaded throughout the city and eventually the nation, the event ignited one of the first major campaigns to dissolve racial segregation, led by the Rev. Dr. Martin Luther King, Jr. The thoughts that must have been transpiring in Rosa Parks' mind at the moment she decided not to give in truly represent the incredible nature of a human being's inherent ability to transcend the influence of exterior forces and build a new reality based on deep personal convictions.

There are many people whose stories are just as extraordinary. Lance Armstrong, Helen Keller, Christopher Reeve, Mahatma Gandhi, and the fifty-six men who penned the Declaration of Independence are all examples people who recognized the capacity of their minds and did not submit to outside forces that attempted to seize control of them.

This was such an empowering thing for me to learn. The remarkable part was my realization that I had the potential to duplicate what I had learned from these great people to address the problems in my own career. Recognizing the power inside this knowledge, I assimilated and applied it where I could and when I could, a piece at a time. Through doing so, some really amazing changes began unfolding in my career. This chapter will show you how to do exactly the same thing.

Assume Command

Taking your destiny away from the Corporation and placing it in your hands begins with assuming command of your most outstanding asset. What is this asset? Your mind. You have the ability to control and direct your mind to the extent that the level of confidence in yourself and your abilities vastly outweighs the layoff threat an employer holds over you. I am speaking specifically about your belief in your own talents and your ability to apply them.

> *Your entire professional future depends on the convictions you hold concerning your talents and capabilities.*

Those convictions hinge upon the thoughts and feelings in your mind. Therefore, the first step to take is to realize that you do in fact have absolute influence over your own mind. Pause for a moment and consider the following: Your mind is the one thing in this world that you do absolutely control, beyond the shadow of a doubt. It is you, and you only, who has ultimate say in what goes on inside your mind.

Furthermore, the realization and acceptance of this truth will empower you to begin creating a concrete conviction in yourself and your abilities that permits unlimited access to the tremendous power and creativity inside you. From this power and creativity you can derive the answers to solve the most difficult problems and challenges. When you practice command over your mind, you will eliminate destructive beliefs and behaviors, such as inadequacy, ineffectiveness and inefficiency. As a result, you will beat the odds, eliminate worry from your thinking and feel an unquestionable sense of certainty in your ability to achieve professionally.

Let's apply some contrast and take a look at the opposite of "commanding your mind" for a moment. Think back to my story at the beginning of Chapter One. I experienced fear and panic on the deepest levels through my reaction to my company's layoff announcement. The fear went unchecked, driven by the outside event that had given it life. This fear grew and spread because it was given constant attention and thought energy from my mind. Had I continued to visualize the end of my employment, I am certain it would have happened. Why? The constant focus on fear fueled it with such power that I experienced it physically, polluting me to such an extent that my ability to take action had almost turned to stone. This all came about through my neglect to control and direct my own thoughts.

Had I not changed my entire focus when I did and taken action, my job surely would have been axed. Case in point: It is absolutely necessary to learn to take possession of your mind in order to avoid being laid-off. It is easy to see that the initial importance of commanding your mind is gaining the ability not to panic when you are under fire.

By learning to properly command your mind, you become capable of sustaining and increasing the flow of income in your life through your own talents despite what challenges may arise.

To get the footing required to create the professional circumstances you desire, a strong foundation inside your mind must be constructed. The idea of not getting laid-off starts in your mind first before it works its way into the world. It is my purpose now to share with you the specialized knowledge I used to journey from fear to conviction, which was the starting place of all my efforts. For you and your *LayoffShield*, this journey begins by holding a deep appreciation for what you already possess: your brain and the mind within it.

Your Incredible Power Source

Let us evaluate the major asset you currently possess at this very moment: your brain. The physical neural-electrical network that is inside you is an astounding biological machine, and is more advanced than any computer on earth. Inside your brain there are over one hundred billion nerve cells, called neurons, which work to form an infinite neural universe that is active night and day. What do neurons do for you? Think of the neurons in your brain as individual colors on an artist's palette. When connected with one another in specific combinations, they paint a picture in your mind, thus allowing you to "think." Research shows us that each neuron in your mind is connected to between 5,000 and 200,000 other neurons, creating a near infinite number of possible thought combinations. *Pause for a moment and ponder the last sentence.*

Driven by the same power that forges lightning bolts in a thunderstorm, your brain generates more electrical impulses through its neural network in a single day than all the telephones in the world. Using a hundred billion signals over a neural network built from several hundred trillion neural connections, it would stand to reason that your human brain is built for more than just day to day existence. Through focus and self-direction of your thought process, you are capable of doing and achieving so much more than you may currently believe to be possible!

The Infinite Power of Your Mind

Although modern technological advances allow us to continue to unlock the secrets of the brain, the mind inside it is beyond the ability of science to quantify. It is in the unimaginable capacity of your mind where the real power lies. The vast majority of people neglect this power, because there is no formal system of introduction to it. What is inside every human being is a phenomenal system of such stamina and capacity that no limits exist regarding what it can truly accomplish. It is the recognition of this force which you possess, known to you as your mind, that is the first layer of armor on your *LayoffShield*.

What is this power? It is a power that only the human species has the privilege of ownership. It is the power of limitless thought and the ability to deny biological instinct and create our own destinies. It is the unique capability to imagine, and to take that picture from the imagination into the realm of the real world. This capability to create what we want in our lives defines us and is extremely remarkable in every aspect. This is especially true in the professional arena. The capacity to create within your mind any thought you choose is a privilege that supersedes the control of any other influence you will ever encounter.

Building your *LayoffShield* involves changing your mind from being driven by random outside circumstances into a tool of will through which you create your own ideal circumstances driven by your personal desires. This is accomplished through the realization and acceptance that your exposure to the everyday environment has a profound influence over your mind. You must possess the courage and wisdom to reach inside your own mind and seize control. Instead of permitting your mind to run rampant with worry when confronted with a challenging situation, you must consciously override the negative thinking and envision a new reality for yourself.

Who defines your capability for you? Who sets the bar for how much you can succeed professionally? Before answering this, you must understand that the person who holds the *LayoffShield* must accept responsibility for their own career and no longer place blame on other people or circumstances. Embracing this belief will take all the power away from others and place it in your own hands. It allows you — and only you — to define the capability of what you can and cannot do. You define this capability based on what you believe.

Belief is Everything

Recognition of the powerful influence your core convictions have over your abilities as a human being is a key factor in gaining command over your mind. Author W. Clement Stone uses the term "social heredity" to describe how through various points of our life experience, we gradually and unknowingly adopt the beliefs of others as our own. The problem with social heredity is that many of the beliefs and convictions we pick up are highly limiting and actually work against us. The worst part is that most adults never stop to question their beliefs. Instead, the belief system most people adopt from social heredity is used to govern critical decisions concerning career and life choices.

Negative and pessimistic convictions concerning our capabilities constitute very limited career options. This is because our convictions ultimately govern our actions. It's a fundamental truth. Would you even apply for a job if you *believed* that you could not get it? Would you compete in an event if you felt that you were not good enough, or believed that you had no chance of winning? Fact: Negative beliefs and convictions limit both our choices of, and chances for, success.

Activate the REAL POWER in Your Mind!

Activate the REAL POWER in your mind by making a diligent effort to explore your past conditioning, specifically what you believe you are capable of and why you believe it. You must place yourself beyond the psychological influences of other people, both from the past and in the present. This is the first fundamental step forward. How exactly is it done? By taking an inventory of any and all self-imposed, personally restrictive ideologies, and questioning those convictions. The following is a five-point blueprint that will help you take command of your mind and unlock the power inside you. Here is the starting point. This is a challenge I am giving to you.

Get a pen. If you did not borrow this copy of *LayoffShield* from a friend or a library, go ahead and write in the book. If you are more comfortable using a journal or a notebook, please feel free. However, you will need a pen to continue.

Step 1: Examine your own beliefs that place low limits and boundaries on your professional abilities. Then write them down.

This is a list of any thought you hold that hinders your capability in the form of a mental barrier. These are referred to in this book as Career Inhibiting Beliefs. I'll share some of the Career Inhibiting Beliefs I discovered within myself, so that you have an idea of what Career Inhibiting Beliefs look like.

I used to believe, without a doubt, that

- The economy is bad and there are no jobs in Information Technology.
- I will never amount to very much professionally.
- There are too many people in my field with better skills than I, therefore that I do not stand a chance.
- Because my college education is not complete, I will not even try to apply for higher level jobs.

Now it's your turn: Write out your own Career Inhibiting Beliefs.
(Be honest here, you have nothing to lose!)

_____

_____

_____

_____

_____

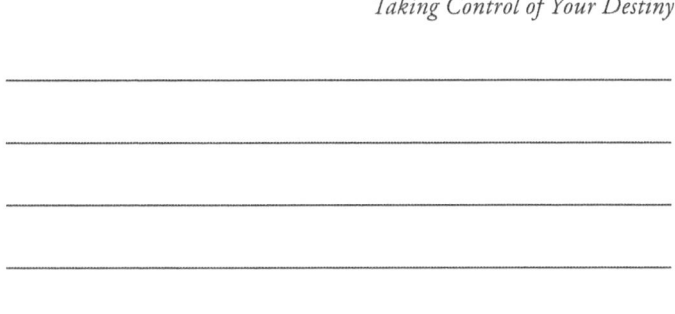

After I completed step 1 of this exercise, I realized that my own Career Inhibiting Beliefs came from many different places: people in positions of authority, relatives, friends and through constant exposure to the news media. All of the Career Inhibiting Beliefs on my list represented an even larger belief that outside influences completely controlled my career. My first list was actually much longer than what I listed in this book; the beliefs above were just some of the major ones that really seemed to be getting in my way.

Step 2: Make a definite decision to no longer allow this career inhibiting belief system to govern you and your efforts.

When I say "make a definite decision," I mean to dig to the Latin root of the word *decide*, which means "to cut off." You must make an active, conscious choice to cut off those Career Inhibiting Beliefs from yourself. You cannot eliminate a lifetime of limiting beliefs in one shot. This exercise requires a continuous and consistent effort that takes time.

Research proves the best way to sever a detrimental belief from your mind is through employing the principle of repetition. Repetition is both effective and powerful.

Consider the following: athletes incorporate repetition into movement to build muscle. Teachers use repetition to increase the memory retention of their students. The old adage, "Practice makes perfect" is true, because practice is repetition. It is amazing how something so simple can do so much.

If we peek under the hood for just a moment and see what repetition is actually doing in your brain, you will clearly see why the concept is sound. Every time you engage a specific action, whether it is learning to speak a new language, playing a musical instrument or just shooting hoops, the portion of your brain in charge of performing that function literally grows! Your brain builds onto its own neural network. This is like a spider strengthening the integrity of its web by weaving onto it over and over again. The new connections in your brain created from repetition provide supplementary neural links as well as increased bandwidth for electrical signaling; hence, maximizing the actual thought power that is available.

For this exercise, we are using repetition to cut away limitations and lay the framework of a new belief system. Okay, without further delay, here we go! Get ready to push that pen deep into the page and write out this powerful statement on the following lines no less than ten times:

I control my own destiny and have faith in my ability to accomplish any goal I set for myself!
(Or write something similar that feels better to you).

_____

_____

_____

_____

_____

_____

_____

_____

Be sure to sign your name after your statement. The space provided in this book is not the limit. To engage the full effectiveness of this exercise, say it out loud! With feeling! Also, for the next three weeks, continue to write your Declaration _daily_, on a fresh sheet of paper until it is firmly embedded in your mind.

Step 3: Construct new convictions as the governors of your mind, convictions that permit no boundaries where your professional abilities and talents are concerned.

Step 3 is a kind of "mental alchemy." There are no boundaries. Realism and logic are not required here. The capacity to aim high, combined with your imagination, are the necessary ingredients. Begin by using information from the first list you made as a base model for this new list. However, in this step, you will write down the counterpart of what you found before to use as your starting point.

After each new conviction is created, begin a diligent search for facts, motives and commitment to back it up, writing everything that supports the new belief directly underneath it. To help guide you, I have provided you with several of my own examples.

I replaced this old Career Inhibiting Belief:

The economy is bad and there are no jobs in Information Technology.

With this new Career Empowering Conviction:

The economy is functioning and there are jobs in Information Technology. I will find and secure more stable employment, as my family depends on it.

NOTE: When I wrote the above statement during the downturn in 2001, I sought out and listed all the ways the economy was working. I looked at all the giant retail stores still doing business, the hundred million credit card transactions taking place daily, digital communications between corporations, and all of the ways the United States economy was functioning with technology. I compared the current economy to the great depression that began in 1929. As bad as all the newspapers were portraying the current economy to be, it did not approach the disaster level of economic crisis the country faced in the early thirties. Shifting my own perspective was an immense help in getting started. I knew that people's needs still needed to be met and they needed technology to do it. There was proof of that everywhere. I based my new belief on that proof and not on the newspaper headlines. I then proceeded to take action using this new belief as a basis for that action.

Following are two more examples.

Old Career Inhibiting Belief:

I will never amount to very much professionally.

NOTE: I had to explore this more in depth before I could properly replace it. I had to dig deep, and it did not come right away. When I did find it, it made perfect sense. I remembered that when I was much younger, my older brother used to joke with me often about how I'd end up living in the basement of his house when we grew up. He told me that I'd be mowing his lawn for him to make my living. I was not as quick-witted as he, and this was the basis of the jokes. My future basement dwelling was the family joke for a while. It seemed that whenever I'd talk about the future around him and his friends, he always told me I'd be his yard-boy. This was bad for me because I unknowingly based my future ambitions on what my brother had told me. It was not a conscious choice really; it was more how I felt about my capabilities. I really looked up to my brother and I believed what he said without question. He did not intentionally sabotage my self-worth; however, I permitted his joke to define me for a time.

New Career Empowering Conviction:

I will be the best at what I do and excel to great heights professionally.

NOTE: When I realized that I was not, nor would I ever be my brother's yard-boy, I knew that it was up to me to choose how far I could go professionally. This conviction was backed up with a written statement that looked like this:

I recognize and acknowledge that I possess unique and powerful talents. To avoid being laid-off, I commit to use all of the talents and skills inherent in me to pursue and obtain a more stable employment, permitting no gaps in my income. I demand daily action of myself toward this target.

That would have been very difficult to accomplish had I not addressed my next mental career roadblock.

Old Career Inhibiting Belief:

There are so many people in my field with better skills, that I do not stand a chance. My college education is not complete, and because I do not hold a college degree, I should not even try to apply for higher level jobs.

New Career Empowering Conviction:

Employers will value me because I value myself. I have strong industry experience, a diverse skill set to offer, and an unrelenting work ethic. I believe in myself and my abilities.

NOTE: This new belief became my launch pad. From this foundation I began my pursuit to uncover all of the assets I thought employers would desire for their top candidates. I had to lock myself into a quest to improve and diversify myself, seeking specialized skills and qualities that would make me a more valuable employee as a whole. I had to stop worrying so much about what other people were doing and just concentrate on doing what I needed to do to conquer the looming layoff threats. I had nothing but my family's faith in me, and faith in myself to back this new conviction.

Now it's your turn. I've provided space for three examples. But don't let that stop you. Extend your writing to a notebook if you need to. The important thing is to keep going until you run out of old Career Inhibiting Beliefs.

Old Career Inhibiting Belief:

_____

_____

_____

_____

_____

_____

_____

New Career Empowering Convictions:

_____

_____

_____

_____

_____

_____

_____

_____

_____

_____

Old Career Inhibiting Belief:

_____

_____

_____

_____

_____

_____

New Career Empowering Convictions:

_____

_____

_____

_____

_____

_____

_____

Old Career Inhibiting Belief:

_____

_____

_____

_____

_____

New Career Empowering Convictions:

_____

_____

_____

_____

_____

_____

_____

_____

_____

_____

Before we move to step 4, I would like you to know that it took a conscious effort and a sincere desire on my part to seek out the things inside me that were holding me back mentally. It was not the easiest task in the world for me to evaluate myself, as well as question a lifetime of beliefs. Although somewhat difficult, it has proved to be of an extreme benefit not only to me, but to my family and my future as well. Locating and replacing Career Inhibiting Beliefs is a strong starting point. What you do with them is the determining factor of how the future will unfold.

Step 4: Create an Environment of Greatness to cultivate your new convictions so you can engage your true potential.

What is the Environment of Greatness? In short, it is a highly effective method of re-educating your subconscious mind. The "environment" itself is your home, your office, and any other place where you spend a significant amount of time. The concept is simple. You design and place elements in your Environment of Greatness that act as constant positive advertisements to your subconscious mind. The underlying principle behind this step is to use self-suggestion, with repetition, to induce powerful changes in you and your career.

Why use an Environment of Greatness? The governing force with which our subconscious mind commands our actions is much stronger and more dominant than anyone would like to admit. Often, we don't even realize why we make some of the choices we do in our careers, but believe me, there is a governing force behind those choices. There is absolutely no question that the beliefs and convictions hidden deep inside the subconscious mind are powerful. To fully maximize the limitless potential necessary to become the masters of our careers, we need to harness this power in the subconscious and direct it toward definite ends. There is one key fact that stands out above any other, and it is this fact that makes the Environment of Greatness an extremely powerful tool for you:

Your subconscious may be cast into any mold, trained to accept any belief, and will learn exactly what you tell it.

Information enters into the subconscious mind in one of two ways: one, extreme fear, or two, through the use of repetition. There is no fear in a LayoffShield, so we will use repetition.

Your own Environment of Greatness

The elements that comprise your Environment of Greatness may be whatever you like them to be, remembering the new list of Career Empowering Convictions you have just written acts as your point of destination. Your Environment of Greatness must include material that invokes a strong positive reaction in you; and your Environment of Greatness should change your state of mind to confidence when you are experiencing it.

Give yourself a belief system that holds a far greater capacity than the limitations learned through social heredity.

Your belief system should be chosen and built by *you*. So then, what exactly do you put in your Environment of Greatness? Here are some ideas:

- The list of your new Career Empowering Convictions.
- Any core convictions you feel are necessary for your success.
- The exact job title you desire and the yearly salary you can envision for yourself.
- Portraits of people who you believe are great; people that inspire you and people who bring out the best in you.
- Include any pictures or drawings that represent the things you really enjoy doing. *(Feel free to cut pictures from magazines)*
- Place empowering quotations where you can read them everyday. *(Because inspirational quotes are very powerful and effective, I have provided some examples on the next page).*
- If you are a music lover, your environment should definitely include music! *(Music is probably the number one method of changing dull moods into feelings of joy and confidence)*
- Begin your day confident. Grab your alarm clock, (*you know, the one that greets you with the horrible and annoying electronic buzzing sound every morning*), and throw it in the trash! Replace it with a CD or mp3 alarm clock and wake up to an empowering song instead.
- Buy a scale model replica of the kind of car you've always wanted to own, and put it on your

bathroom counter. *(Own the car in your mind first, and then you will come to own it in your life.)*
- There are no limitations to what you can do. Use any elements you feel are necessary to supercharge your subconscious!

I have been using the Environment of Greatness for several years now and its effects have been far-reaching. Through daily exposure to the elements within my own Environment of Greatness, my mind began to feel a sense of truth about the messages that were being constantly being shown to it. Over time, the new beliefs embedded themselves deep inside me. What had begun as ideas written on paper became solid convictions. These convictions, which I designed, are the governing force behind my thought and actions.

Being the chief designer of my own belief system enabled me to aim higher. Through aiming higher, I was able to attain goals that I previously believed not possible. One such goal was attaining the position I hold today. Before I recognized and *believed* in my own potential professionally, I never once imagined myself holding the title of Network Architect and earning a respectable salary. In fact, there was a time not so long ago where it would have been incomprehensible for me to even imagine it. *The belief had to come first*, before the job or the salary. This belief grew from a single idea into the powerful governing force through cultivation from my own Environment of Greatness!

As promised, here are some examples of quotes I have used to create a powerful Environment of Greatness for myself:

"I was conceived to accomplish, built for success, and gifted with the seeds of greatness."
-Zig Ziglar

"I have the courage to aim higher."
-W. Clement Stone

"Never ever, ever, ever, give up. Never give up!"
-Winston Churchill

"I now have enough time, energy, wisdom and money to realize all my desires."
-Shakti Gawain

"I will not let myself be laid-off"
-Chris Henson

"I am the master of circumstances."
-Napoleon Bonaparte

How long before the Environment of Greatness makes noticeable changes in your career? It is little a different for everyone, but it really boils down to just three things: The first is the level of effort you place into designing your Environment of Greatness. The second is the amount of time you spend in your Environment of Greatness. And, the third is the amount of faith you choose to place in yourself. Although I began to experience results within a few months of use, I still employ the Environment of Greatness everyday to keep my mind properly tuned. Now, it is your opportunity to be creative. By taking action now and re-building your current home and office into an Environment of Greatness, you are setting yourself up for unparalleled professional success! Go for it!

Write down some ideas for your Environment of Greatness:

_____

_____

_____

_____

_____

_____

_____

_____

_____

_____

_____

_____

_____

_____

_____

_____

Step 5: Construct a Mental Firewall System to protect your mind from negative influences.

The next time you go into the lobby of a large bank, take a good look at the vault door. Examine it closely. Look at the over-sized hinges, the massive deadbolt and the intricate locking system. Use that picture of the massive bank vault door in your imagination to give life to the idea that you have an impenetrable place inside yourself where your ideas and beliefs will thrive, completely invulnerable to the negative influences that exist in the world. You know that your mind is a valuable asset. It is the most valuable asset you own. Like any asset, it must be protected. It must be protected from two formidable enemies, fear and worry, who are constantly attempting to gain access to the precious resources inside.

Enter the Mental Firewall

A Mental Firewall operates on a similar premise as a computer or network firewall. That is, it blocks harmful outside influences from gaining access to the resources the firewall protects. The Mental Firewall protects your mind from the fear of being laid off, so that you may deal with a layoff threat with confidence and precision. The Mental Firewall is your best defense against stress and workplace rumors. It prevents negative influences from attacking your concentration and poisoning your attitude.

The Mental Firewall is a basic thought process you can put into action any time you want. It is simple. When you recognize something negative, such as the nasty remarks of a coworker, simply think to yourself, *"I am going to Firewall that!"* As soon as the coworker has finished speaking, drop what was said out of your mind by consciously re-directing your thoughts to a new point of focus!

The Mental Firewall makes perfect sense when you think of what actually occurs on a physical level. Your brain uses electricity to 'think' and give expression to thoughts. When you divert your center of attention away from a negative suggestion over to a completely different thought, you are taking electrical energy that would normally fuel that negative thought and cutting its power supply. This is much like unplugging an appliance. You render it powerless.

How do you make the Mental Firewall work? The key is to have your mind prepared when outside forces test your Firewall. You have to be ready to redirect your thoughts. The best way to be ready is to choose a focal point that is extremely significant to you personally; a focal point compelling enough deserve the 'top-spot' in your mind. It can be anything you like, but again, I stress that it must be strong and represent something about which you feel deeply. Once you select your "goto" focal point, you're ready! That is all there is to it!

I remember one day, a few years back, (when I was first learning to use my Mental Firewall), someone had tossed a newspaper on one of the tables in the company café. The newspaper headline read: '4000 more jobs cut!' A group of my coworkers were standing around the table, discussing the headline. I clearly remember hearing one of them say, "There are no jobs for anyone in technology." Immediately, I refocused my thoughts onto my son, Jacob. I thought about how fascinated he was with the airplanes we had both seen the weekend before. I replayed highlights of our weekend at the Air Show in my mind. I kept to myself and I did not stop to talk with the people at the table. After a while, I refocused my thoughts on constructing my resume and the companies I would send it to that afternoon. Now that I think about it, that day in the café had not crossed my mind until I shared the experience with you just now.

Okay, now it is your turn to discover your powerful focal point to use in your Mental Firewall. Where are you going to redirect your thoughts when people test your Firewall?

_____

_____

_____

_____

_____

_____

_____

_____

_____

"I am going to Firewall that!"

That is a very powerful statement, isn't it? The daily use of the Mental Firewall strengthens the command you have over your mind, as you are making a conscious choice of where you direct your thoughts. You are taking away the power other people have to influence your thoughts, emotions and beliefs. Because the Mental Firewall is a learned thought process, you must make it a habit to work effectively. Practice, practice, practice and the Mental Firewall will be a valuable layer of armor on your *LayoffShield*.

SUMMARY

Build the foundation of your LayoffShield through the five-point blueprint for gaining command over your mind:

1) Seek and write out your existing convictions that suggest or establish low limits and boundaries on your professional abilities.

2) Look at the list you created and make a definite decision to no longer allow this career inhibiting belief system to govern you and your efforts.

3) Construct new convictions as the governors of your mind — convictions that permit no boundaries where your professional abilities and talents are concerned.

4) Create an Environment of Greatness to cultivate the new convictions from seedlings into oak trees, engaging your true potential.

5) Construct a Mental Firewall System to protect your mind from negative influences.

Finally, Embrace Confidence.

As you move to the next chapter, remember what you have learned about your mind. Come back to this chapter again and again, for the magnificence of the human mind is a truth. Use this truth to embrace confidence. Know that confidence is a mental attitude through which your thoughts are free of doubt and disbelief because your mind is focused on a greater purpose: This greater purpose vanquishes fear and puts your mind to work as your ally. When your mind is fully engaged as your ally, there is no barrier that cannot be surmounted.

"All the problems become smaller if you don't dodge them, but confront them. Touch a thistle timidly, and it pricks you; grasp it boldly, its spines crumble."
-Admiral William S. Halsey

CHAPTER THREE

Learning to Anticipate Intelligently

Is it really possible to predict a layoff far enough in advance so that you can take the right action to avoid it? Absolutely, yes. Do you remember the movie *The Karate Kid*? In it, there is a memorable piece of wisdom that has stayed with me through the years. This is the part of the movie where Mr. Miyagi tells his student, Daniel, "*Best way avoid punch; no be there.*" Although Mr. Miyagi's words were in reference to the art of Karate, the wisdom he relayed holds true with any threat. The best way to avoid being laid-off from your job is to not be there when it happens.

Inside the limitless capacity of the human mind — in your mind — lies the ability to anticipate and react. You do it everyday already. If you drive a car or navigate your way across a busy street, you are constantly anticipating the moves of other people and reacting to them with extreme accuracy, adjusting your timing, re-calculating your position and trajectory with split-second timing, avoiding danger gracefully. You may be doing this hundreds, if not thousands of times each day without ever even thinking about it. This is an extraordinary ability. This layer of armor on your *LayoffShield* will sharpen your powers of awareness and intuition when it comes to dodging the swinging axes.

The precision and intelligence that unlocks this awareness are acquired through the use of the Four Keys. These Keys are used to unlock a chest that contains a treasure map. What is on the map? First, this map will reveal the location of "layoff landmines" so you may gracefully step around them. Second, the map will also reveal a direction for you. This direction is a path toward the rewarding, high-paying, secure position within your field of expertise – your treasure!

The Four Keys are each specific, focused actions. As you read and learn about the Four Keys of Anticipating Intelligently, keep in mind your own professional destination point, whatever this may be for you.

Without further delay, I now hand you all Four Keys as well as accounts of their real-life success, followed by an empowering set of questions to help you determine your short-term vulnerability to a layoff.

Key #1:
Have a Burning Curiosity for your Profession

This key is the real desire in you to actively search out emerging business and technology-driven changes that could potentially affect you, your company and your specialized field of expertise.

If you're going to be able to predict whether or not your job is in danger, you must have a burning curiosity for your profession. Curiosity is what drives the human spirit and is the seed of all future successes. Curiosity is also the prequel to action. The amount of desire you take with you to this task will be in direct proportion to the amount and the quality of the information you uncover.

Seek information about your company, your industry, your trade, your competitors, your field, and anything else that relates to your career as a whole. If your desire to avoid a layoff is strong, then channel that emotion into initiative. When your mind is really heated with the desire for answers, they will come, and some may even appear from the least expected places. Begin by obtaining a project notebook to keep your information organized. Always Be Seeking! In a world where information truly does move at the speed of light, finding clues that empower you to predict significant industry changes may be only a few mouse clicks away.

NOTE: *Later in this chapter, I have written a list of questions you may use as guidelines for your search.*

The success of your predictions depends largely on actually confirming that the information that you do uncover is indeed accurate. You must be able to separate facts from fiction. Make your approach scientific. Validate clues and facts through corroboration from multiple sources. Be sure your sources of information are genuine; and extend your trust carefully. When you do find a helpful piece of information, question the source's intent for publishing that piece of information. Is there another motive there? Do not let anyone do your thinking for you. Your own powers of deduction and anticipation are strong. Rely upon your own judgment for the final say.

"We have a hunger of the mind which asks for knowledge of all around us, and the more we gain, the more is our desire; the more we see, the more we are capable of seeing"
-Maria Mitchell, American Astronomer

Key #2:
Keep a Wide-Open Mind

Maintaining an open mind toward all possibilities, while recognizing and assembling the facts and information about your own career field, allows you to predict events intelligently. Look where you are now and rate yourself on the level of opened-mindedness you feel that you have now.

There is nothing more destructive regarding one's professional success than to have a closed mind. Have you ever known anyone like this? Someone who is so fixated on their own way of thinking and doing things that no new ideas are ever let in? They are completely unprepared for change because they have adopted an attitude of close-mindedness. Maintaining this frame of mind can cause a person to blatantly ignore a coming tidal wave, and render them incapable of gathering the facts necessary to see the wave coming. People who have embraced a closed mind are often overwhelmed by new major industry moves and are enveloped in confusion. Do not let this be you.

Grasping this key and using it means setting aside all preconceived opinions and known ways of doing things and completely opening your mind toward new ideas and information. By allowing your mind to consider more possibilities, you will widen the array of information you will use. The beneficial result is a more intelligent map upon which to base your predictions. Once you have made a strong effort to open your mind, you will find that the number of opportunities to advance will increase significantly. Take this key and use it to unlock the doors of your mind. When those doors swing open, you will see new possibilities where others see none; you will make friends where others see enemies, and you will empower your career to a degree far greater than you have previously imagined!

"There is no reason anyone would want a computer in their home."
-Ken Olson
Chairman and founder of Digital Equipment Corp, 1977
(This quote from Ken Olson, reminds us how important an open mind can really be.)

Key #3:
Embrace Change

Accept change when it does come, predicted or not, seeing and fixating only on the ways it will benefit you.

Although some changes seem to carry a negative meaning on the forefront, using this key means you must dig in deep and search for all of the ways to make change work for you. Should you map out a possible major change on the horizon, as you probably will, see how you can make that change an ally and not an enemy. Use what you find as a means from which to benefit your career. Carve a path with the knowledge you uncover by setting aside the negativity and doubt that can often accompany large changes. Again, focus only on the ways that change will benefit you.

For instance, if your company is abandoning a legacy system or process where you hold expertise, use the change as an opportunity to become the authority on the new system. Sure, it is a lot of extra homework and effort on your part; however you will be rewarded for your application of this key through continuous job security.

How does positive fixation on change act as your *LayoffShield*? Positive fixation on change makes you visible throughout your company as someone who is aligned with the goals of the business. This is powerful because the majority of people tend to complain when a change is forced upon them. They pull the covers over their head when changes are near, or adopt a stance akin to having their arms crossed in front of them. Their only hope of stopping the coming change is their own unwillingness to embrace it. Perhaps these people believe that wishing it will go away will somehow make it so, and the company will go back to the way things have always been done. This is a lose-lose situation. These people are the first to become the least valuable to their employer as they are obviously not traveling in the same direction as their company. Their attitudes are reflected in their actions, and their negative outlook becomes crystal clear to the company and everyone in it. They are layoff targets.

Take this key and tightly integrate it into your thinking toward the future. Don't immediately buy into the negative propaganda that crowds adopt concerning the changes that affect them. Remember to use your Mental Firewall when dealing with negative people. Do your own thinking and fine tune that thinking into the question, "*How can I benefit from this?*" If you truly seek the answer to that question, the inherent intelligence that resides in your mind will give you an answer. As the holder of the *LayoffShield*, you will find ways to make change benefit not only you, but also you will find ways to make it benefit your bank account, and eventually you will make it benefit the ones you love.

"Change is the law of life. And those who look only upon the past or present are certain to miss the future"
- John F. Kennedy

Key # 4:
Use Your Conviction to Fuel Action

This last key is imperative to making the other three work; without it, all the knowledge in the world will do you no good. This key is *action*. When you have all of the facts, and a direction is laid before you, construct a plan of action that is built entirely under your own influence and intelligence. Your plan should be one that reflects a positive career move, yet it also should be built from your research on industry direction. You may choose to develop a specialization in your field, go back to school to learn a new trade, or perhaps you may want to provide a new service that you see will be needed in the future. Your abilities are infinite. You live in a wonderful country where you are free to set your dreams into motion and achieve them!

When getting ready to begin your new plan of action, permit no thoughts in your mind except ones that inspire courage. Share your plan with only those people who truly support you, and protect your plan from those who would ridicule you. Write your plan down and place it where you can see it daily. Understand that any significant plan of action takes time, so don't feel frustrated when results don't happen as fast as you'd like. *Just keep going.* I recognize that last sentence is easier for me to say than it is for you to do and I have an appreciation of the work it takes to see a plan through. Here are some ideas to keep you moving along the way that have worked very well for me. These ideas are based on this fact:

Heightening your desire for something motivates the action behind it.

1. The Environment of Greatness, described in the previous chapter, is one way to heighten your desire again and again over an extended period of time. You can do this by placing elements in your Environment of Greatness that reflect the outcome of your plan. If you are training to be a CPA, write your name followed by the letters, CPA and pin it up. If you want to work for a specific company, put your name next to that company's logo and pin it up where you see it everyday.

2. The support and belief of those closest to you is another key ingredient in sustaining both desire and action over time. Your closest friends are valuable assets; their belief in you and your abilities can have very powerful effects.

3. Visualizing where you want to be is also very effective for keeping action going over an extended length of time because visualization disciplines your mind to think and act in terms of "success." It teaches your mind to already possess that which you seek.

4. There are further instructions, which will render valuable assistance in helping you transform your desire into its real-life equivalent, in Chapter 10.

Regardless of the method you choose, never stop until you get there. You can do it!

"In any moment of decision the best thing you can do is the right thing, the next best thing is the wrong thing, and the worst thing you can do is nothing."
-Theodore Roosevelt

A Real-Life Success Story Using the Four Keys

PART ONE: Formulating the Plan

Traveling back in time once more, this time to the winter of 2001, I was determined to find a brand new employer, as the company I was with seemed to be sinking quickly. I visited all of the Tech Job Fairs at major venues and hotels around the city. During one particular Job Fair event, I remember walking in and standing at the top of the stairs, and just being amazed at what I saw. I looked down onto the event floor, and it was jammed with hundreds of desperate candidates, all of them waiting in line with resumés clutched in their hands. I had no idea that my career field was saturated with such steep competition. Most of these people had probably been standing in line for hours, just waiting to submit a resumé at a single company booth, hoping for a chance to talk to a recruiter. My eyes re-focused on the resumé I was holding in my hand. My only thought was this: *How am I going to make myself more valuable to potential employers than all of these other people?*

What was it that would make me win? To ensure my name would not ever appear on a cut-list, I had to have something that all of these people waiting in line did not have. To get the edge I so badly needed, I knew that I had go outside my own experience and see my industry through a broader perspective than I ever had before. Although I knew my current job was in danger, I was really searching for a more permanent solution to the problem. I had to make my *LayoffShield* impervious to the inevitable threats I would face in the future.

In order for my skills as a Network Support Specialist to be highly valuable, they would have to meet the needs of companies in a very big way. What were those needs? What would determine them? It was the burning curiosity I held for my own field that led me to the first answer. I knew that it was the types of technologies and equipment large companies were investing in now that would determine the support needs those companies would have in the future. This one simple economic fact was the base from which I launched all of my research. I needed to know: Who was purchasing technology? Why were they purchasing it? What kind of technology were they purchasing? Who manufactured the most purchased technologies and equipment? What would the person supporting the special technology need to know? More specifically, what skill set would they have to have? How many people had (and will have) that skill set?

My desire to get the answers I was seeking was indeed definite, as the competition I would face in the future was nothing less than steep. I needed to answer the questions so badly that my mind had developed a strong sensory acuity for the information I was pursuing, tuning in to anyone and anything that could help me. This even meant learning from certain people I did not like personally, as their professional expertise was more valuable to me than maintaining my own ego. I had to have an open mind to what it was they had to say. Although a sense of tension existed, the people I approached with questions gave up answers willingly. The knowledge I received in exchange for my pride was well worth the effort, as it would prove its worth to me in the two years to come.

After I really started searching, information just seemed to find its way to me. I read through piles of technical publications that contained interviews and insights from people who were considered to be leaders in the networking world. I carefully read what they had to say and gave my thought to their opinions. I looked at new high tech products and the markets they were poised to penetrate.

A good friend saw what I was doing and he took it upon himself to instruct me in the vast realm of the stock market. He did this not so that I could get rich through picking some fantastic stock; instead his basic instruction led me to great web sites that contained enormous amounts of information about the companies I was researching. I evaluated every clue I had uncovered, looking for commonalities from different sources as to the direction of networking technology in the industry as a whole.

When the answers came, it was as though the sluice gates had suddenly opened up and answers flooded my mind. I had more info than I knew what to do with and it all seemed to point in one direction. I had begun this search with one definite objective and I had now discovered a "cutting-edge" technology which I wanted to employ as my new area of specialization. It was called, Voice over Internet Protocol, or "VoIP". My decision to pursue the support aspect of VoIP was based on my anticipation that this technology had a very high potential of being embraced by literally thousands of companies in the near future. Why did I think that? What made this specific technology so special?

Simply this. It could save money. The idea behind Voice over IP is to allow a company to place long distance telephone calls using their existing private data network, (instead of the public telephone system). The obvious benefit was that large corporations would be able to save millions of dollars in their communications bills by completely bypassing long distance carrier tolls. Because the potential inside this technology to save money was so great, I felt it would be used abundantly very soon. If this were true, then support needs for it would also be in high demand. The other great thing I discovered was that there did not seem to be very many people who had adopted Voice over IP support as their specialization. This was a major industry change and I wanted nothing more than to ride the wave. This was the right choice for me. I knew it. Now, how do I make it happen?

The technology's top vendor had developed a rigorous certification path for willing candidates. The certification path consisted of many hands-on style classes that covered the technology in depth. Once I knew what I wanted, I mapped out the specific certifications I would earn to increase my value in the marketplace and found the classes I needed to take. The roadmap I designed for myself listed a combination of different certifications that would mix well for my specialization. This was it. Okay, now what?

Although I was very excited that I had discovered a new career path for myself, the decision to pursue it meant dedicating a good portion of my spare time to the in-depth study that becoming an expert would require.

Making this choice meant leaving my comfort zone and grasping for something that was well beyond my present understanding. Although my background and current position had elements of network support, learning this new technology meant beginning again from square one. It also would require a significant investment of my time and money, both of which were in short supply.

Things became more difficult when I discovered that the certification classes cost thousands of dollars each, (and I had mapped out six of them). Where would I get the money I needed? Even if I did get the money, when would I take the courses? Most of the training centers offered classes only during standard business hours, which conflicted with my work schedule. The real icing on the cake was when I found out that the pass rate for the certification tests was very narrow, with few people gaining a passing score on their first attempt. I could not imagine expending all the effort and not achieving a passing score. I felt as though my train had come to a dead halt only a few feet away from the station where it had begun its journey. All of a sudden, the great career path discovery I had made seemed to be too much effort and trouble. Was VoIP training really worth all the effort, time and money?

This decision was a major pivotal point in my life. I believed I had found the right path for myself professionally and I had to move forward, even though I did not know how I was going to accomplish this seemingly insurmountable task. Had I made a choice other than to proceed forward, my future would now be *very* different. Although I had no idea at that time the significance of that choice, I did know that my wife and son had placed their faith in me. It was this faith that would not allow me to lose sight of my goal or quit. It was because of my family that I had given myself no method of retreat. I had to figure out a way. I just had to.

How exactly did I do it? That answer, along with 'Part Two' of this story is continued in Chapter Eight. For now, I want to tell you what happened to me as a result of my decision to proceed with the plan. My efforts paid me two-fold. First, the specialization that I acquired allowed me to out-maneuver two other layoff rounds that would come in 2002 and 2003. I did avoid that lethal punch, twice. *Thank you, Mr. Miyagi.* I would not have been able to do that unless I was extremely attractive to a new company at a time when competition was fierce. Second, the decision I made to act on the career enhancement plan I had chosen, derived from my use of the Four Keys, has brought me a secure and highly prosperous position in my field that I still hold to this present day.

You may ask, what do I mean by "secure"? There is a paradigm in the professional world today, "that there is no such thing as job security anymore." I don't believe that. I'll tell you why. For me, being secure is knowing that should some completely unforeseen event occur where my employment with one company is suddenly severed, my skill set would be in such high demand, that I could quickly sell it and myself to another employer. Being "secure" is the conviction that I am able to meet a specific need and provide a necessary service to any prospective employer through my skills — a set of skills that was designed through an intelligent anticipation of the needs and direction of my career field.

Anticipating Intelligently in the Short Term

Your ability to Anticipate Intelligently will also benefit you in the short term, given that you seek and use all the variables put forth to assess threats to your employment. Although the same Four Keys still apply, a different set of questions must be answered to give you accurate, useful information. In performing a short-term prediction of this type, you must really keep your eye on what is going on around you. I offer you a very effective set of questions that will be of great help in anticipating whether or not you are vulnerable to a layoff threat. When you read these questions, answer each one with full diligence. Gather the most accurate information that you can, remembering fully that the more specific information you acquire, the more intelligent choice you can make.

By answering these questions you can determine:
- the general direction of your industry, career or trade
- your immediate vulnerability to a threat
- the likelihood of that threat affecting you in the future
- a direction or path to take professionally, using the full strength of your *LayoffShield* to serve you

For ease and organization, the questions are divided into three parts:
1. Corporate Acquisitions and Mergers
2. Paradigm Shifts
3. You and your perceived Worth to Your Company

1. Corporate Acquisitions and Mergers

As you begin to do the actual research and uncover answers to these questions, keep in mind that you are seeking patterns that are pointing in a particular direction. Regardless of that direction, you will benefit, because you will be able to act in advance. Again, feel free to write in the book.

- Has your company made any acquisitions in the last 36 months?
- If yes, why do you think there was an acquisition? What do the companies that were acquired all have in common with one another? What would your company have to gain or lose?
- Have other companies in your line of business been making any aggressive acquisitions? If yes, what do you feel they are specifically trying to accomplish?
- Have there been any shifts of upper personnel, re-organization or "streamlining" in your company? What about in competitor companies?
- Has your company undergone an auditing process in the recent past?

(NOTE: Streamlining and auditing are often attempts to make a company more attractive by straightening out the books and other aspects on paper before a merger can take place.)

- What is your company's financial status? Financial history?
- Is your company being 'eyed' by a larger company for potential merger?

(For this next question, put yourself in the CEO's or CFO's shoes; think this through as if you were the boss.)

- If you suspect an acquisition or merger is near, look at the other company, specifically duplication of your department in that company. Examine it. How efficient is that department? If you were an Executive, and you had to choose between the two duplicate or redundant departments, which one would you choose and why?

2. Paradigm Shifts

Here you will seek a potential change in the way companies think about the way they do business. Paradigm shifts often overwhelm many individuals, as massive changes seem to come from "out of the blue." In reality, most significant shifts in business practices and thinking are evident long before they are actually implemented and accepted. They are evident only to those who actively seek them out and are constantly tuned into all aspects of their career.

- Have there been any operational shifts in your field of expertise or industry? For instance, other companies adopting new technologies or practices that are re-defining the business model?
- Can you identify the company who is the leader in your professional classification or your company's line of business? What has made them the leader?
- What has that leading company done in the last two years? Is there a pattern present in their actions that could indicate a large change in business operations, affecting the industry as a whole?

- Is there another company poised to surpass the present leader?
- Is there a new technology or software that is more efficient, that saves enormous amounts of money; that could affect the operations within your company, eventually affecting you?
- Looking with the highest perspective you can adopt, in which direction is your industry headed? What factors play a defining role in determining your company's present course?

3. You and Your Perceived Worth to Your Company

Have you ever tried to evaluate a situation from another's viewpoint? In this search, it is imperative. When you approach the answers to these questions, use a CFO's perspective of recognizing vital business components within the company.

- How many people in your own company are proficient in your specific skill set?
- What do you actually produce for your company? Are your efforts known beyond your immediate department?
- Are your job and duties duplicated anywhere within your company?
- Realistically, do you feel your role in the company is indispensable? Why?
- Does your company outsource any of its operations?
- What is the morale of the people who are running your company?

- How does your supervisor's boss view you? Above that, their supervisor?
- Looking at your group/division/position within your company through a CEO's eyes, how would they view it? Is it of extreme importance to business operations? Is it completely unknown to them?
- Do you see your group/division/position as heading in the same direction as the company and the business itself with regards to business practices and efficiency?
- If your company for some reason had to quickly cut spending, cut budgets, where would they do it first and why? Where would they do it second? Where would they do it third?

Answering all of these questions to the extent necessary to help you will take plenty of time and effort, no doubt. If you enter your workplace with the sincere desire to get all of the answers, you will possess a sensory acuity for the information you seek, and the knowledge will flow toward you more quickly. You may also find other valuable information beyond the scope of what is asked here, as the questions here are designed as a starting gate for you; they are not meant to be a set of rules or restrictions.

SUMMARY:
THE FOUR KEYS TO ANTCIPATE INTELLIGENTLY

Key #1: **Have a Burning Curiosity for Your Profession.**
This key is the real desire in you to actively search out emerging business and technology-driven trends and changes that could potentially affect you, your company and your specialized field of expertise.

Key #2: **Keep a Wide-Open Mind.**
Maintain an open mind toward all possibilities while recognizing and assembling the facts and information about your own career field, allowing you to predict events intelligently.

Key #3: **Embrace Change.**
Accept change when it does come, predicted or not, seeing and fixating only on the ways it will benefit you.

Key #4: **Use Your Conviction to Fuel Action.**
When you have all of the facts, and a direction is laid before you, construct a plan of action, make a decision and immediately act on it!

"Think as you work, for in the final analysis, your worth to your company comes not only in solving problems, but also in anticipating them."
-Tom Lehrer, Harvard Professor

CHAPTER FOUR

Becoming an Indispensable Asset to Your Company

What is it that makes an employee an indispensable asset? What makes someone so valuable to their company that their name never shows up on a cut-list? I sought the answers to these questions more than anything else at the beginning of my journey. It was my burning desire to get these answers. Through very intense research and life experience, I got them. And I used them. It was this knowledge, heading the top of the list in this book, which enabled me to secure my employment while the massive layoff tornado ripped through the Technology Industry. This chapter and the information in it will prove to be a most valuable and profitable tenet, should you choose to incorporate it into your thinking and ultimately into your life.

In answering the two questions from the previous paragraph, you must know that there exists a substantial number of unwritten elements that comprise a major portion of an employee's worth to a company. These elements are not university diplomas, certificates or even the professional background one must possess to be proficient in a career. They are not letters of recommendation, nor are they qualities that are normally listed on a standard resumé. What are they?

The elements of which I speak are the human traits and outstanding personal qualities that define us. They are the kind of qualities that cannot be purchased by anyone, as their value supercedes any imaginable dollar amount. They are the kind of qualities that are not taught through our formal system of education. Most companies do not offer training to obtain them, yet the person who possesses these attributes is of extreme value to every employer. Forging the fourth layer of protection onto your *LayoffShield* is learning the value of these elements and how to use them profitably. Please allow me to introduce you to the Six Outstanding Personal Qualities.

Outstanding Personal Quality #1:
A Positive Mental Attitude

Why is a Positive Mental Attitude so valuable to a company? I will explain. Employers today are aware of the quality of the service their employees give on a consistent basis. Raises are based on it. Promotions are determined by it. And cut-lists are built from it. Whatever it is that you do for a living — whether you talk with customers, build homes, write software or manage people — the level of quality you place into your work is highly visible to others. The same holds true for the kind of service you give to others. The quality and the service that are inherent in the work you do are the two most important traits you have to offer an employer. The driving force behind high quality work and outstanding personal service is a Positive Mental Attitude. A Positive Mental Attitude is the only foundation from which high quality work may be built and a Positive Mental Attitude is also the only characteristic that can induce a person to give the most outstanding service to their customers.

Now, the people who run successful companies understand and recognize the importance of high quality service. Corporate leaders know that the better service they are able to give their customers, the happier those customers will become. Those customers will then generate more business for that company through repeat transactions and through word-of-mouth advertising. When a high customer satisfaction index is attained, companies make more profit. Profit is what all eyes see. The more profit a company is able to generate, the larger they can grow their customer base. The more customers they are able to serve, the more profit they are able to make and thus the cycle repeats itself, getting larger each time. Starbucks Coffee Company is a fine example of this principle in action.

These same leaders who operate highly successful companies also know that the quality of service their company is able to give to its customers is based completely upon the mental attitude of every single employee in that company. They know that their company's success is directly linked to the attitudes of the people in it. This is why a genuine Positive Mental Attitude is such valuable commodity.

It is not only a valuable commodity to a company, but to you as well. For example, let's say that layoffs are the only remaining alternative for your employer, and your Management must decide who goes and who stays. There are many aspects they must consider before moving forward with layoffs. There are the obvious factors that come into play, such as the necessity of your position, the value of your skill set, and cost of the maintaining your position. However, there is one more factor. This fourth factor resides within the emotional realm of the decision maker; as a decision is often based upon the choice that will mean the least amount of displeasure for the person doing the deciding. This fourth factor is the quality of the experience you leave behind with other people. It is the lasting impression that your bosses, your co-workers and the people throughout your company have about you. This impression is based on two types of communications:

1. Direct: interpersonal conversation. (*face to face, or telephone*)
2. Indirect: (*e-mail communication, reputation and word of mouth*)

This is called the "Personal Impression Factor," and can weigh significantly when your job is hanging in the balance. Which way the scale tips depends entirely on you.

Let's say for a moment (hypothetically, of course) that your attitude at work was mostly negative. This would, of course, work against you. Why? This negative mental attitude is projected from you through a combination of signals; some are conscious, some are subconscious. You send off signals through facial expressions, hand movements, body postures and even through your physical proximity to the listener. These signals are broadcast by you during conversation and then register in the brain of the listener. More than 60% of your communication is non-verbal. Even when you are speaking, your tone of voice communicates more than the specific words you deliver.

The real damage that is incurred through having a negative attitude is that permanent experiences (or impressions) are left in the minds of others about you. This is often referred to as "having a bad taste in your mouth" about someone. Even if a person has a skill set and knowledge that is essential to their company, when they possess an attitude that produces a strong emotional reaction of dislike in others, eventually, that negative person will be let go. There is no avoiding it.

On the other side of the coin, let's say you are an employee who demonstrates the traits of being positive. You are an employee who is pleasant, friendly and you inspire authentic kindness in the people with whom you come into contact. It is evident to others that you enjoy your job. Now, the communication signals you broadcast are working <u>for you</u>! These signals become "seeds of goodwill" when received in the minds of other people. These seed impressions you leave with your co-workers and management act as positive reference points when your name pops up. Imagine the opportunities that can sprout from positively sown seeds. (NOTE: *Body language and non-verbal communications are covered more in depth for you in the next chapter.*)

Tuck this key fact into a safe place in your mind: When building your *LayoffShield*, the Personal Impression Factor (based on a positive mental attitude) is *imperative* to your continuance and success with your company.

> *"A positive attitude is a person's passport to a better tomorrow."*
> **—Anonymous**

Outstanding Personal Quality #2: Honesty

In your relationship with an employer, any employer, Honesty translates directly to Personal Accountability.

Personal Accountability may be defined as what you do when you know that no one is looking over your shoulder. If you did not have a Supervisor or Manager who takes account of all the tasks you perform at work, would you still do them? Would you do the minimum amount required, taking breaks often and breezing through the day with minimal effort? Or would you perform your work as though your Manager were right there?

Looking at the same idea from another angle, if you ran a small business and you placed all of your heart and soul into that business, what kind of employee would you like to have working for you? Would you want someone who had absolutely no Personal Accountability helping grow your company? Would you want to *pay* a person like that? The employer's perspective is a lot different, isn't it? Using a small amount of contrast, as we have done here, it becomes clear why, for employers, Honesty — Personal Accountability — is a must-have quality.

In the eyes of an employer, the higher an employee's Personal Accountability is, the higher their productivity will be. The importance of employee productivity, on a company's list, is second only to profit. It all boils down to productivity; either the company is getting it from its employees, or it isn't. Why is it so important, really? The lack of Personal Accountability can cost a company a pretty penny. For instance, if your company is one of 500+ employees, and each person is paid the equivalent of $20 per hour, and all 500 employees goofed off just one hour a week, the lost time would total $10,000. Over the course of a year, that number would grow to more than half a million dollars of lost profit.

Build a strong Layoff Shield: Demonstrate Honesty

Honesty is demonstrated to your employer through the most simple of ways. The foremost is taking full responsibility for your own actions concerning your work and your duties to your employer. Give credit to others when you are commended personally for what actually may have been a team effort. Keep your word with co-workers and customers alike. When you tell someone you are going to do something, by all means, do it. Never try to fill the gaps in your knowledge with guesswork and half-answers. This is especially true in interviews. It's okay if you don't know something. Do the research and follow up later with the answer. Above all, practice Honesty as a core virtue of your professional lifestyle.

> *"I have found that being honest is the best technique I can use. Right up front, tell people what you're trying to accomplish and what you're willing to sacrifice to accomplish it."*
> **-Lee Iacocca**

Outstanding Personal Quality #3: Loyalty

Off all the characteristics that comprise the perceivable value of an employee, Loyalty is the one that is most representative of the strength of the alliance an individual holds with their employer. It is this devotion towards one's company that has become quite rare in this day and age. The days of spending a career-life with one company seem to be in the past. The benefit in this, however, is the more rare loyalty becomes, the higher its value to an employer. Why is it so valuable?

The value of loyalty is far more than the cost of the time and resources to constantly train new employees. Loyalty's value is even greater than the amount of financial pain felt by companies plagued with high attrition rates. An employee who feels the existence of this professional bond is incorruptible and holds a feeling of integrity about their position. An employee who demonstrates dedication, honesty, and trustworthiness is one who is first and foremost, loyal to the company that employs him. Loyalty is the pride felt by both the employee and the employer as a result of their alliance with one another. It holds further value for a company by leveraging this important fact; many customers will only purchase goods and services from people they like or people with whom they feel comfortable. A loyal employee is that familiar smiling face behind the counter or pleasant voice on the phone that greets the returning customer by name.

How do you make this work for you? Loyalty is a two-way street between employer and employee, so a company must compensate its employees to be loyal through providing benefits, incentives and an environment that cultivates loyalty. Although this is true, as a holder of the *LayoffShield*, you will want to tip the scale slightly in your favor by always giving a little more in return to your employer than you receive. You will want to engage in acts of support for your company. There are many ways, but we will explore some of the more basic modes of action, and from there you can use your imagination to further benefit your cause and add to your *LayoffShield*.

Never slander your company to anyone, even if your closest co-workers are doing so. In fact, do just the opposite. Up-sell your business and your company to people with a sincerity that reflects that you really do feel that way. Tell customers how glad you are to work there. Demonstrate your commitment by attention to detail. For instance, after you have completed your portion of a project, follow up with the team implementing the next phase to ensure they have everything they need to be successful. This shows your loyalty to the project, the team and the company.

If your plans are to stay with your company, be definite about that with your Managers or Supervisors. Use the opportunity of a performance review to demonstrate clear plans that you do, in fact, want to stay with your company. If your company has clothing with professional embroidery of their logo, buy it and wear it. Display any performance awards or 'years of service' awards in plain site.

Lastly, weave the spirit of Loyalty into the work you do, focusing on the good attributes that your work does for others and how you have helped your company. Doing so may inspire loyalty in others who had little or none, exponentially increasing your own value. When you assimilate the strategies in *LayoffShield* for creating and demonstrating loyalty, be sure that you are doing so only if you are coming from a place of genuine spirit. None of the preceding actions I have mentioned are of value unless you truly do feel some sense of loyalty toward your company.

"I'll take fifty percent efficiency to get one hundred percent LOYALTY."
-Samuel Goldwyn, American Film Producer, Founder, MGM

Outstanding Personal Quality #4: Willingness to Serve

There is nothing in this world that will bring you more personal profit than the willingness to serve others. Serve others? Yes, absolutely. The term "customer" is all too often defined as a person who comes to a store and buys something. The people who provide "customer service" are serving the person who comes into the store. These definitions are narrow and limiting. If you wish to use the full effectiveness of your *LayoffShield*, you must redefine who the customer is. The new definition is short and simple. Everyone is your customer. Every human being is entitled to the same common courtesy and level of eager service we normally reserve only for the people who are willing to hand their money to us.

It will be very profitable for you to begin thinking of your co-workers and all the people you communicate with throughout your day as your customers. Think of them as though your income depended upon the level of service and courtesy you provide them. And it does. If you map out how your role connects to everyone else's roles in your company, you'll find what I am saying is indeed true. Using this new definition for the term "customer" helps you provide outstanding service when you may not be in the mood to do so. Simply by saying, "he is my customer" or "she is my customer" will change the way you feel about helping that person. It will cause you to ask yourself, "What is the best way I can support this person?"

How exactly does this add armor to your *LayoffShield*? Throughout the tens, hundreds or possibly thousands of people with whom you communicate daily, your courtesy and sincere desire to help them solve their problem will define you as someone who is genuinely supportive. It will clearly define you because so few people are doing it. These types of actions echo very loudly throughout a company and can generate kudos and "thank you" letters to your manager or above. If you keep on connecting the dots, I am sure you can see that adopting a willingness to serve will also generate opportunities for career advancement, opening doors that you may have never known existed.

You can also have fun with it. You can individualize how you relate with each person. This not only livens up your job, but it provides your customers with a positive unique experience each time they speak with you. All people have something in common in this world of ours. Find it and engage in a bit of light talk before jumping down to the matter at hand. When you talk with someone, use that person's name frequently throughout the conversation. A sincere tone of voice conveys your willingness to help. Use the common vocabulary of a courteous person, "I appreciate it," "thank you," "do you mind helping?" "please," "your help is greatly appreciated". These are all powerful phrases that crown the service experience with class. Again, you are more than welcome and highly encouraged to place your own spin on it. Remember to be courteous in everything you do and say and others will take notice. Due to the rarity of this important quality, you will win every time that you demonstrate a Willingness to Serve.

"Everybody can be great... because anybody can serve. You don't have to have a college degree to serve. You don't have to make your subject and verb agree to serve. You only need a heart full of grace. A soul generated by love."
-Martin Luther King, Jr.

Outstanding Personal Quality #5:
Personal Initiative

Personal Initiative boosts the *LayoffShield* the same way nitrous oxide boosts a racing engine. There is no quality more favored by any individual who manages or supervises other people than Personal Initiative. Why? It is the simple fact that when an employee engages Personal Initiative within their professional environment, they lesson the amount of "management" they require. This person does not have to be told what to do and is always busy, even when the workload is light. Although the obvious benefit is crystal clear, we have not yet begun to delve into the real value that Personal Initiative generates for a company.

If you reflect on Chapter One for a moment, you will remember that I was threatened by the large layoff axe swinging closer and closer to my neck. After I decided to stop worrying and do something about that threat, I spent a significant amount of time looking for answers, answers which I could use to arm myself with the protection I needed to avoid the upcoming round of job cuts. The first answer I unearthed was using the practice of taking initiative. It was the idea of doing something significant to help the company without being told to do it. That is what I did.

Remembering the big company announcement that frightened everyone, I recalled that as part of their initial layoff speech, the crowd was told that company-wide sales lacked horribly. I thought about my company's problem. There was really not a way I could directly generate revenue of any kind, as my job with that company was purely one of technology support. Our entire group was considered more of a company expenditure and did not generate revenue in any way. We had nothing to do with the sales side, and the company's problem was for the marketing people to resolve. At least that was the consensus among my group. I, however, did not agree.

During the same time all of this was happening, I received a call from my older brother. He told me that the company he was working for in Colorado was going to open up several new locations in the Dallas area, where my family and I were living at the time. My brother shared with me that his company was currently building a new store in Dallas and that many new stores were also planned for the area. You'd think I would have immediately connected the dots, but I didn't. My thoughts were more of humor during the phone call, and I think I offered my basement to him if he wanted to transfer to Dallas.

Two whole days passed, and it was not until very early in the morning on the third day that my brain connected my brother's phone call to a possible sales lead for my employer. I knew that any new stores being built would need business phone systems and possibly networking equipment.

I took a good portion of the morning and carefully constructed an e-mail to our VP of Sales. In the e-mail, I introduced myself and enthusiastically relayed this possible sales lead, telling our VP that I wanted to help and that I thought this lead could generate revenue for our company. Finally, the e-mail was complete and I read it back to myself. I almost didn't send it. Fear enveloped me and boldly attempted to prevent my taking action. I was not on the sales team and the VP of Sales had no idea who I was. Being so far up the corporate ladder, he would probably wonder why some guy from support was sending him an e-mail. "Maybe I really don't have any business doing this," I thought to myself, as lead generation was far beyond anything in my job description. All of a sudden, the idea seemed stupid. Inside, I knew that was not true. I fought the fear, but it held on like someone who does not give up in an arm-wrestling match, even when their wrist is just inches from the table. I finally won and forced the hand of fear down. "No, they need this lead." I clicked *send* and off the e-mail went!

The very same afternoon, I received a reply to my e-mail. My stomach still felt a little wrenched as I opened the reply e-mail and read it. What I saw completely astonished me. It was a thank you note from the VP of Sales, assuring me that he'd follow up on the lead and that he appreciated my e-mail. Although his reply was short, it was powerful. It was powerful because he'd 'cc'd' three other people in his reply: my boss, his supervisor and lastly, the Division Vice President. I believe this single act of Personal Initiative is what saved my job, as the first round of layoffs swept through the company just a few short weeks later and I was not among those who were let go.

As your eyes move past the words on this page, I would ask that if you take only one thing away from this experience I have shared with you, let it be this; No one told me to write that e-mail. I just did it. When you engage in Personal Initiative, be sure to temper it with reason and intelligence so you choose to act upon the correct endeavors. Don't be limited by your job description regarding what you can do for your company. Arm yourself with the outstanding trait of Personal Initiative and vastly expand the effectiveness of your *LayoffShield*.

"You can't build a reputation on what you're going to do."
-Henry Ford

Outstanding Personal Quality #6: Drive

How can Drive increase the strength of your *LayoffShield*? To properly answer this, we must first define what Drive is. Drive, simply put, is the tenacity with which you tackle your job. It is the force that compels you to move forward to increase your talents and abilities through using them every day. It is the desire to out perform everyone in the crowd and rise above. Drive is concentration on opportunity. However, I believe that Drive is so much more than all that.

Drive escalates your value to an employer through allowing your company unlimited access to your full potential and talent. It boosts your worth; because through Drive, you can actually help your company grow. Can one person's Drive really do this? I offer the example of Lee Iacocca.

What made Iacocca so successful? He was able to use the Drive he possessed like an engine to continuously assert his talents and motivate others to see his vision. It was this amazing quality that moved him from being just another worker in the clutch-spring department at Ford Motor Company to becoming the mastermind behind the 1964 Mustang. Note: *Ford continues to use elements from Iacocca's original design to this very day. Just look at the 2005 and 2006 Mustangs.*

Iacocca's incredible Drive accelerated his rise to greater heights after Ford Motor Company had fired him. Using the end of his job at Ford as an opportunity instead of a setback, Iacocca's Drive compelled him to go to work for

Ford's ailing competitor, Chrysler Corporation. Chrysler benefited dramatically from Iacocca's leadership and innovation. It was Iacocca's hands that pulled Chrysler out of its financial tailspin and aimed it toward the clear skies of profit through the ingenious creation of the Minivan product line. Yes, one person really can grow a company through Drive.

How does Drive benefit you?

The largest and most evident benefit is that possessing Drive allows you to achieve the goals you set for yourself. Drive allows you to increase your effectiveness in solving difficult problems through ensuring your constant forward motion toward the solution, no matter what obstacles you encounter. Holding true in any profession, the ability to work difficult problems through to a solution on a consistent basis greatly increases your level of value to those that employ your services. Because there are so few people who are considered real problem solvers, tapping into Drive and combining it with your action, is a great way to separate yourself from the average performer. This obvious distinction from those whose ambitions and Drive exist in the realm of mediocrity tempers the armor on your *LayoffShield*.

To benefit from Drive, there must first exist an understanding on your behalf that the potential power of Drive is fueled entirely by the amount of opportunity you envision for yourself. Drive is linked to your perspective; your insight as to what defines an opportunity, as well as, your courage to embrace it. The tremendous power of this quality is unleashed when you make the decision to use all you've got as a means to move yourself forward, based only on your own belief that you will get there. This vast quantity of energy can be transformed into an idea you have for your company, a plan to better your position in that company or a career move toward a new company.

How do you tap into Drive then? Earlier, I mentioned that Drive could be defined as concentration on opportunity. It is this intense concentration on any desire, idea or target that acts as fuel for Drive. Allow me to illustrate for you.

Imagine that you traveled back in time one hundred and ten years. You are standing inside the Engineer's cab of an iron steam driven locomotive. You grip a wooden handled shovel and stab the scoop into a pile of coal rock in the tinder car behind you. With all your muscle and effort you shovel coal into the sweltering firebox of the engine. After engaging the throttle, you feel the wheels of the train slip and then suddenly engage the track. The massive train protests, but slowly lurches forward. With each pile of coal you muscle into the inferno, the heat from the firebox grows more intense. The super-heated steam forces the train to move faster and faster beneath your feet.

Continuous positive concentration of your thoughts on the plan you are developing is much the same as keeping the firebox loaded with fresh coal – Except for one thing. The tinder car only holds so much coal, but you have an unlimited supply of focus and concentration.

Use Drive in all of the work you do. Use it to complete your tasks with the due diligence and attention to detail they deserve. Use it to get the job done right the first time. Use it to dig out the solution that you know exists. Using Drive this way makes for a high quality product.

Just look at the '64-'66 Ford Mustang. See how many of those cars are still on the road today. This same quality can be integrated into anything, as your exact profession does not matter where Drive is concerned. Use Drive to ensure your every customer gets a high quality product. Drive will not go unnoticed. In fact, others, who also employ this powerful quality, will recognize it and may put in a good word for you when you need it the most. This makes Drive an indispensable component of your *LayoffShield*.

The Power of the Six Outstanding Personal Qualities

You have just learned how each of the six outstanding personal qualities will shield you when the layoff axes swing. When you fully engage what you have learned here, your actions will lead you toward significant career advancement. The extent and the level to which you make use of the six outstanding personal qualities in your professional world will determine precisely the rewards you will experience in return for your efforts.

However, I have one quick word of caution for you. There are companies in existence today that neglect the intrinsic value of every one of the six qualities, companies who treat their employees with disregard and a lack of respect. Through some miracle unknown to me, these poorly run companies manage to remain in business somehow. I imagine that companies such as these are only able to turn a profit due to their customers' high tolerance for severely degraded service. Regardless, it is up to you to recognize if, indeed, you are working for one of these unworthy companies and immediately take appropriate measures.

Because you work hard for the money you earn, be sure you are rendering your quality service to the right people. If after some time, your genuine efforts are never acknowledged, and you are treated unjustly, it then becomes time to fire your employer. Yes. Remember, you have this power in your hands. I freely acknowledge (again) this is much easier for me to tell you than it is for you to do. However, finding the right job could be the single greatest gift you ever give yourself. The right job does exist. Your career or job should match your own talents to some extent, and the higher that extent, the happier you are and the easier it becomes to use the Six Qualities.

After I had consciously sought out the elements from which to forge my *LayoffShield*, I realized that I had actually used a few of the elements from the Six Qualities before in my career. One event in particular comes to mind. I would like to share a true story with you. This single event became the bridge that would take me from a minimum wage position to the high-salaried realm of the technology industry. It was the catalyst that began a chain reaction of great things to come my way professionally. It all began with a single opportunity. I did not receive this first opportunity because of my knowledge or passion for computers. In fact at that time, I knew nothing about computers.

The Low Man on the Totem Pole

In the spring of 1996, I worked for a local electronics retailer in Littleton, Colorado, as a Customer Service Representative (CSR). Working in this position, I tended the front counter of the store, which entailed working the cash registers, greeting people as they came in the door and helping customers who were upset from time to time. The person in the CSR position was often considered to be the low man on the totem pole, as any other position in the company required a college degree or equivalent experience. I really didn't mind. Although this was not my ideal career, I really liked working one on one with people and being around the latest and greatest electronics, and this combination made the actual work I had to do rather pleasant.

I actually had a lot fun as a CSR. There was always a lot of joking going on with co-workers and customers alike. It was the upset customers who were a little trickier to handle. However, they all had one thing in common — they all had a story to tell. Sometimes it would take manager involvement to satisfy the complaint. Other times a sympathetic ear would remedy the situation. On several occasions I was able to take an upset customer and transform their experience by relating to them and identifying with their problem. In certain situations, joking with them a bit and taking the seriousness out of their problem would have them smiling before they left the store. After a while I began to enjoy the challenge of transforming an angry customer into a happy one.

I had no idea at that time that I was being silently observed. In fact, I did not become aware that my performance was being monitored until much later, when the store had encountered a minor crisis on a busy Saturday morning. The store had placed a full-page computer sale ad in the newspaper that day and none of the computer sales specialists had shown up to work. Rather than calling one of our other locations and requesting that one of their computer sales specialists be sent to our store, the senior manager, Larry, asked me if I would like to go out on the floor and sell computer systems. He did this, knowing fully that I had no knowledge of computers.

You'd think I would have jumped right on that, but I had a great deal of apprehension about selling computer systems. I knew there would be an onslaught of unanswerable technical questions from possibly hundreds of customers. The feeling of not being able to answer any kind of technical question, whatsoever, left me feeling awkward, nervous and just downright uncomfortable. I really did not want to do it.

Although everything inside me was telling me to decline immediately, for some reason that I cannot explain, I couldn't say no. "I'll do it," I told Larry.

I'll never forget that Saturday. It was one of the busiest days that store had seen. Inside the retail whirlwind of madness, something really amazing happened. All of the people who had questions about computer systems were actually patient with me and sympathetic to the store's unforeseen crisis. They waited for me while I vigorously called Computer Sales Specialists at our company's other outlets to see if they had the answers I needed. The day flew by furiously; I talked with one customer after another, again and again, until nine hours had passed. Somehow I had made it through the workday.

As we locked up the store that night and headed toward our cars, Larry took me aside and placed his hand on my shoulder. He thanked me. He told me that I was the best solution for that crisis because of my willing attitude to help people. Larry told me that it truly did not matter that I lacked the technical expertise to be selling computers that day, and that he had chosen me because of my ability to provide outstanding help to customers with an uncommon positive attitude. I could not believe it. I was even more shocked when he offered me a promotion to Computer Sales Specialist that very same evening.

That day changed the direction of my career completely. Within weeks of accepting the position, my pay had tripled, because the computer systems I sold paid a hefty commission. (It was a good thing too, as I found out I was going to be a new Dad around that same time.) In the months that followed, the company provided me with professional training, equipping me with everything I needed to be an expert in selling and supporting small home office computer systems. I enjoyed this new position more than I had anything else I had ever done. This enjoyment must have reflected in the work I did, because in just twelve short months, I was again offered a promotion, this time to computer sales manager at the company's flagship store.

As I look back on the events in that period of my life, where my career was just beginning to build momentum, I know for a fact that the opportunities that were given to me were based solely on my attitude and willingness to serve people. Knowledge and expertise did follow, but they were more of an effect of the opportunity, rather than the actual cause of it. It is difficult to contemplate where my career would be now if I had said "No" that day instead of "Yes."

SUMMARY:

THE SIX OUTSTANDING
PERSONAL QUALITIES

1. A Positive Mental Attitude.
    PMA is imperative to your continuance and success with your company.

2. Honesty
    Honesty is the core virtue of your professional lifestyle.

3. Loyalty
    Weave the spirit of loyalty into the work you do, focusing on the good your work does for others.

4. Willingness to Serve
    There is nothing in this world that will bring you more personal profit than the willingness to serve others.

5. Personal Initiative
    Personal Initiative boosts the LayoffShield the same way nitrous-oxide boosts a racing engine.

6. Drive
    Drive escalates your value to an employer through allowing that company unlimited access to your full potential and talent.

CHAPTER FIVE

The Most Valuable Skill

It was the summer of 2003. The phone rang. After the caller had introduced herself — a representative from the company I had recently interviewed with — I listened intently. After a few moments, I clenched my hand over the bottom of the phone handset and yelled out loud, "Yeeeeeaah!" I had just been made an offer that I could not believe. My entire body was electrified with excitement. After a few moments, I regained my professional composure and placed the phone back up to my ear and spoke. "It would be my pleasure to accept your offer. Thank you." I had just been offered a salary higher than I had ever earned in my life!

The next morning, I experienced the thrill all over again when a big red and white FedEx envelope arrived at my door. I ripped open the top, grabbed the papers inside and tossed the torn envelope on the floor. It was now official. In my hand was the written offer letter from my new employer. Seeing the dollar figure on paper literally made my mouth hang open.

Grasping the letter tightly in my hand, I realized that in gathering and using all of my research to protect myself from layoffs, I had also built myself a key. That key had just unlocked the door to a fantastic job for me. It was the extra boost that allowed me to shoot across the finish line and win against hundreds of applicants. I now clutched the evidence of this key's effectiveness in my fist.

This chapter will show you how to make the key work for you. Mastering this key will get you into your next job, or wherever you want to go professionally. It will unlock previously closed doors in your current job, allowing you to succeed and excel. This key is the most valuable skill you can ever have. That's right — the most valuable skill. What single attribute could possibly accomplish so much? What is this key?

It is the ability to inspire trust and confidence in others where your personal communication and business relationships are concerned. It is the ability to invoke an authentic pleasant emotion in anyone. It is the ability to have others see you as someone who is likeable and very easy to get along with. It is the ability to defuse an argument before it happens. It is the ability to motivate other people toward your ideas and thoughts. This is the key of Enhanced Charisma. Enhanced Charisma is, hands-down, the single most important skill you can ever possess in any business relationship you enter *and* . . .it is a skill that can be acquired!

The benefits of learning, practicing and eventually mastering your Enhanced Charisma are endless. I say this because the opportunities that grow from the cultivation of positive business relationships are endless. Connecting with people is the best thing you can do for your career. When the right people are receptive to your plans and ideas, extraordinary things happen. Doors to promotion and advancement are opened for you. Plans transform into reality. Money comes your way.

It is now time to take possession of this amazingly powerful skill and put it into action.

How Others Interpret You

All great actors and actresses are masters of understanding the manner in which they are perceived by their audiences. They are completely aware of how their every nuance and gesture will be interpreted. They use this knowledge to enhance the implication, purpose and flavor of their performances.

Now let me ask you, who is your favorite actor or actress? When you arrive at your answer, think about why that person is your favorite. Most times, the reason you might favor a particular actor or actress may be that you admire the qualities that person possesses; or perhaps you have a great deal in common with a character they portray. It all comes down to this: that actor or actress elicits a pleasing emotion that connects you to them.

Although you and I are not necessarily acting in our jobs, the awareness of how all of the people with whom we engage daily interpret our behavior is critically important. How we seem to ourselves is not necessarily how we seem to others. Activate your awareness to this fact. Begin to reach with your mind to shift your perspective one hundred and eighty degrees and see yourself through another person's eyes. Strange as it may sound, doing this requires some courage, as you must temporarily set your ego on a shelf in order for this exercise to be effective. The first move toward mastery of Enhanced Charisma is to search out all of the ways you can constructively improve the impressions you make on other people.

I'm not talking about how you dress, but rather habits or traits that have the potential to generate negative reactions from other people. Engaging in this self-evaluation will prove to be a huge leap ahead for you. I can guarantee you that very few people are willing and able to view themselves objectively and then do something about it. As I said before, it takes courage. Grab your pen again and let's do a quick brainstorm now.

The idea is to take a simple inventory. Circle Y or N; be honest and *don't worry* if you answer *yes* to any one, or even all of the questions:

- Do you have the habit of interrupting or cutting people off in conversation? Y / N
- Do you find that you have a negative mental attitude at work? Y / N
- Do you find that you are talking about bad news a lot? Y / N
- Do you speak too loudly in your cubicle or workspace? Y / N
- Do you possess the tendency to want to be right all the time? Y / N
- Are you blatantly closed toward other people's suggestions? Y / N
- Are you considerate of other people's personal space? Y / N
- Is it difficult for you to cooperate with others? Y/N
- Do you make it evident that unsolicited interruptions of your work annoy you? Y / N
- Does your phone voice reflect an impatient or annoyed attitude? Y / N
- Do you command or dictate orders to other people without regard for courtesy? Y / N

- Are you difficult to approach? Y / N
- Do you use capital letters in your e-mails as a means to get your point across, communicate anger or displeasure? Y / N
- Are you sarcastic with others? Y / N
- Do you purposely ignore some people? Y / N

Are there any other traits or habits that you use at work that could create negative impressions about you?

_____

_____

_____

_____

_____

Again, please don't worry if you answered *yes* to any of the questions. In fact if you did, it is a good thing because you are being honest with yourself. Commit to doing the task of improving your outward presence and explore yourself through the eyes of others. If you don't know what to look for, seek help. Ask your best friend, husband or wife. When I did this exercise myself, through some tactful questioning, I found out that the people around me thought that I spoke way too loudly on the phone. It seemed that my voice carried, and was disturbing the office environment. It took a conscious effort to dampen my volume and speak in softer tones during my phone conversations. As a result, the people in my area seemed more friendly and relaxed toward me.

After you have finished circling the answers above, reach over to the shelf, grab your ego again. Ego is a good thing. Once you have figured out your own areas for improvement, one by one, go through and wipe out those annoying traits. How? You rid yourself of them through physically engaging in the opposite of the trait you are working to eliminate. If you find you have the habit of talking all of the time, be a listener. Go through a conversation and just listen. If you find that you have been rude, make it a point to be genuinely courteous. You get the idea, I am sure.

The Art Behind Enhanced Charisma

Developing a sensory acuity to other people's thoughts and emotions through learning to read body language is an art. Reacting appropriately and tactfully is also an art. You learned in the last chapter that you and I communicate more information with our bodies than we do with our words. The body language you use defines your true feelings and intentions toward other people. If you have ever glanced through an office window at two people having a heated debate, you knew immediately that tension existed, even though you could not actually hear them argue. You knew this by the way they were using their bodies and their facial expressions. Just from a two-second glance, you automatically knew not to knock on their door.

Before beginning a conversation, we often give some thought to what we will say to people, how we will say it, and even run through possible conversation scenarios in our minds. Very little thought, if any at all, is given to how people interpret the body language display. Body language is a detailed science, and it would take an entire book to properly convey every technique. However this chapter is designed to give you some of the basics, which I know will prove to be beneficial for you when you put them into use.

Using Your Body Language Intelligently

There are two kinds of body language: positive and negative. For the purpose of this book, we can divide these two categories further so that we may best understand and benefit from them. They are:

- Physical gestures that inspire trust and physical gestures that create distrust
- Physical gestures that are of a friendly nature and physical gestures that are of an unfriendly nature
- Physical gestures that relay your sincerity to others and physical gestures that show you could care less about what others say
- Body postures that give off confidence and body postures that show nervousness or fear.

Remember, people will always mentally accept your physical language over your verbal language. This is any physical gesture or sign that you make, consciously or not, that signals to others your real intentions or thoughts. You cannot emit both a positive and a negative impression to others at the same time. That means you are either sending one or the other. Knowing this, we will now take a look at some of the key points in using and reading body language; as well as what you should avoid. Remember that knowing what *not* to do can be equally as important as practicing the right techniques. Let's start with the face and head and work our way down.

Influence others with enthusiasm. There is nothing more inspiring and nothing that has more power to invoke good will in others than using a friendly facial expression when you speak, and delivering your expression with such enthusiasm that there is no doubting its authenticity. You add to that enthusiasm by nodding. Nodding your head while listening to someone else shows your positive interest in them and invites that person to continue talking with you. Always use your smile. A genuine smile combined with the sincerity of continuous eye contact is a powerful signal that immediately tells other people:

- You are receptive to what they are saying
- You approve of them
- You are someone who is likeable

What you are really telling someone through using this body language is that they are important to you. You are telling them that they matter. That is huge! There is no better way to win someone over than to make that person feel significant inside. This is true because you are meeting a fundamental need all people have. You can begin immediately. This may sound funny at first, but practice your smile and practice making pleasant facial expressions in the mirror. To really make this work, you must see yourself the way others see you. The mirror is a fantastic way to practice and it can make a boring elevator trip a little more fun.

Win them over by showing you are open. What you do with you arms while you are speaking (or listening) to someone will clearly define the kind of person you are in their mind. For example, crossing your arms in front of your chest during a conversation tells the other person that you are closed to them, their ideas, and their way of thinking. Crossing your arms is also a defensive posture. Avoid it in business relations with others. Instead, you will want to assume a more relaxed and open posture. If you are standing, relax your arms and let them hang naturally. If you are sitting, put your arms beside you on the armrests of the chair, opening your upper torso. People will instantly become more receptive to you when you practice open postures while communicating with them.

Gain the trust of others. Showing honesty is key in establishing any kind of trust. You do this by keeping your palms open. Open hands, or using gestures where you show your palms and wrists signals honesty to the person you are talking to on a subconscious level. Plain and simple, it shows others that you are not hiding anything. On the contrary, placing your hands behind your back screams you that are covering something intentionally. Pointing is bad, because it implies blame. You will also want to avoid nervous hand gestures, such as rubbing your hands together, playing with your hair, fiddling with things or constantly adjusting your clothing. This kind of movement distracts the person you are talking to and can generate uneasiness in the conversation. Instead, use your hands to motion while in conversation the same way you would use them if you were engaged in your favorite hobby, using motions that are flowing, smooth and unforced.

Reflect confidence in your posture. Your posture is a rather obvious signal to others about your perceived self worth as well as your current emotional state. Have you ever thought about how you carry yourself? Part of gaining the confidence of others in your abilities comes from how you project yourself to them. After all, you would not want to place your faith in someone who does not believe in himself, especially if your reputation is on line, right? It is this primary reason that your body postures, combined with the way you carry yourself, are extremely important in the professional arena. We are often taught through social heredity that having pride and ego are bad, when in fact we need them to succeed in business and ultimately in our lives.

Cultivate your pride by placing it into your body language. Carry yourself with respect and courage. When you walk, keep your shoulders back and chin up, (remembering to be natural) and never look at the ground. Remember to use temperance and balance when displaying pride, so that you may dynamically adjust yourself to reflect confidence and not exceed the threshold into arrogance.

When you are sitting down in a chair, (perhaps in interview situations and other professional situations where people must evaluate you), sit with your back straight and lean in toward the person with whom you are engaged. Leaning toward someone alerts your correspondent to your heightened interest in them and what they are saying, again, making that person feel important. Regardless of whether you are sitting or standing, maintain a confident poise. Practicing confidence in your body language broadcasts your natural strength and ability to other people on a subconscious level. The end result, or personal benefit, is that people will be willing to extend their faith and trust to you.

Match others' communication styles. Your financial gain is linked directly to your ability to induce the cooperation of other people, that is, the cooperation of your customers and your coworkers. (They are one and the same, remember?) To increase your level of success in obtaining that cooperation, when you engage people, your communication technique should be different for each person with whom you come in contact. Why? People will cooperate with you if they like you. Part of your "Personal Impression Factor" in the eyes of another person comes from how you personally communicate with them. A common communication style creates a kind of invisible bond between two people.

People speak with different levels of energy; they speak at different speeds, use different inflections of their voice and move with different styles of body language. It is up to you to identify a person's style and adapt yourself to it by temporarily matching it. When you do this successfully, a person's over-all receptiveness to you will greatly increase. Your chances of getting on someone's nerves will decrease dramatically. This is because you are "playing on their field", all subconsciously, of course. You are speaking their language.

There are also certain situations where your manner and tone must be changed in order to receive the benefit of someone else's attention. As an example, when I began teaching my Network Fundamentals class, I remember some of the first feedback I received from one of my close friends who sat in on my class. He told me that I was speaking to the class like Keanu Reaves spoke in the movie, *Bill and Ted's Excellent Adventure.* He told me that as a teacher, I needed to hold a more professional demeanor and tone of voice. He was right; and I put what he said into action. As a result, my future students ultimately had more respect for me, and my credibility shot sky high.

Read others and react tactfully to them. Have you ever known anyone who just cannot take a hint? Someone who has no respect for your time? I think we all know someone like that. As a result of this person's complete lack of perception, it makes their Personal Impression Factor sink like a stone. Unfortunately, the person who is doing this may have absolutely no clue they are creating dislike in others, simply because they are either ignoring, or not consciously reading the body language of the person with whom they are speaking. Our purpose here is *not* to be that person. After reading this, tune in and watch the signals other people give out during a conversation.

A reliable guide to a person's continued interest in talking with you lies in their feet. Look at the direction of someone else's foot (or both feet), as this is an indication where that person wants to go at that moment in time. A person thoroughly interested in what you have to say will have both feet pointed toward you. Someone who is ready to wrap up the conversation or who is ready to leave may have one or both feet pointed toward the door. Some people may use their whole body in this manner, turning their torso away from you while still keeping eye contact as a means to signal they're through listening.

Other clues a person can give about their desire to end a conversation may appear through a series of smaller gestures. These may be as obvious as a break in eye contact and quickly glancing elsewhere. Or, they may be less obvious, like constantly shifting body position, wringing the hands, or a change in breathing rate. Once you attune your acuity to reading the physical language of others, their inner thoughts will become more obvious to you, and you will be able to react appropriately in any situation. Remember, this type of consideration increases the quality of the Personal Impression Factor you build in other people and stays with them long after the conversation has ended.

Come out on top in phone conversations. Because phone conversations lack the obvious visual input of body language, we must focus solely on the voice. Practice listening carefully to people on the phone and linking their voice inflection to their current mood. Learn to identify another's state of mind through recognition of their various vocal tones and inflection. Knowing the emotional state of the person on the other end of the phone (and reacting appropriately) will help you negotiate more effectively, solicit the information you need and may even get you the favor you need to complete a project.

An important point to remember: Don't let the person on the other end of the phone control you or your state of mind. If the person you are talking to is being snippy or even mildly rude, rather than doing the natural thing and mirroring their tone, take control of the conversation through using this powerful tactic: *React to their harsh tones with a smile in your voice.* When you speak with a smile, your voice inflection reflects that smile and it is immediately recognized by the recipient. Try it and see. If you can keep a pleasant sound in your voice consistently, the other person will eventually match your mood, and the conversation will go in the direction you choose.

The Ace in your Deck: Sincerity of Purpose. Use what you have learned to increase your sincerity of purpose when you communicate in business. This 'Ace in your Deck', sincerity of purpose, effectively communicates the strength and emotion of your ideas to others in such a way that they will understand them and share your passion for them. Successful business <u>is</u> the sharing and selling of ideas at any level. The more effectively you can sell yourself and sell your ideas to other people, the more valuable you will be. The more valuable you are, the higher the reward you will earn and the stronger your *LayoffShield* will be.

"Electric communication will never be a substitute for the face of someone who with their soul encourages another person to be brave and true."
- Charles Dickens -1868

SUMMARY:
THE MOST VALUABLE SKILL

1. Enhance your charisma by taking a self inventory of your traits may that bother other people and eliminate those traits.

2. Use your body language intelligently in conversation.

3. Influence others with your Enthusiasm.

4. Win them over by showing you are open.

5. Gain the trust of others through being open to them.

6. Reflect confidence in your posture.

7. Identify a person's communication style and adapt yourself to it.

8. Read others and react with consideration.

9. Use the Ace in your Deck: Sincerity of Purpose.

CHAPTER SIX

Making Difficult People Your Allies

We've all had to do it at one time or another — bite our lip, hold back frustration and trudge our way through working with someone who is flat out difficult to get along with. Constructing an effective *LayoffShield* involves learning to engage difficult people so that you emerge a winner. There seem to be difficult people at every job, at every level. There are difficult customers. There are difficult co-workers and supervisors. Throughout my career in Information Technology, I have been placed in numerous situations where I had to figure out ways of getting along with some real tough people. My experience with this challenge has taught me that I could not make them go away, nor could I force them to change, *but what I could do was transform them into my allies.* The following eight-step process is an essential enhancement to your *LayoffShield* that allows you to cooperate effectively with difficult people and come out on top.

Step 1
Think Accurately

If you are engaged in a confrontational situation in a professional environment, where you are face to face with a person who is argumentative or disagreeable, you must think accurately. Thinking accurately means to decide whether it is more important to win the debate at hand, or if there is a larger benefit to letting that person win in the moment. Thinking accurately is to maintain control of your emotions and ego in the moment. Thinking accurately is using your Mental Firewall as a means of avoiding unnecessary confrontation and using your mind to render a more profitable outcome. You may avoid unnecessary confrontation through engaging your capacity for forward thinking. In your mind, envision the direction you want the conversation to take and what you want the outcome to be. Most people argue for the sake of arguing, with no destination or desired outcome in mind (aside from just wanting to be right). This kind of argumentative practice is like driving a car with no steering wheel. Can you imagine trying to do that? Instead, when you are in a situation where you must debate someone, always keep your destination point in mind.

ASK YOURSELF:

What direction do I want the conversation to take?
How can we both benefit from this situation?
Can I enhance the relationship with the other person?

To ensure a harmonious future working relationship in the midst of a difficult encounter, remember that the original debate topic needs to be resolved to both parties' mutual satisfaction. Suppose that during your debate, you kept a positive thought in your mind; a thought that focused on building a better professional relationship with the other person as a desired outcome of the debate. By focusing on the positive culmination you seek during an argument, you can neutralize the volatility of a situation by decreasing the level of emotional intensity you are broadcasting. *Use your tone of voice as to extinguish hostility!* Use tones that are soft and warm. Smile and be sincere. The other person will recognize your intent and reduce their own intensity as a result of reading your signals. This technique is powerful in face-to-face negotiations and will prove to be a very useful tool for you.

> *"We shall never be able to remove suspicion and fear until communication is permitted to flow, free and open."*
> **-Harry Truman**

Step 2
See the World Through Their Eyes

To make someone your ally and win his or her trust, you must possess the real desire to see a situation from that person's point of view. Seeing the problem from the other person's perspective may enhance your overall understanding of the entire situation. It will allow you to examine all the possibilities and reach a mutual solution more easily. You gain the perspective of another person by asking them non-aggressive questions that reflect your genuine desire to understand their point of view.

I really want to understand this the way you do. Please tell me why you feel that way?

Your point of view is critical. Please help me to understand it better.

Your point of view is important to me. Please explain it to me in more detail.

Feel free to place your own spin on these questions and use them. Again, when the other person realizes that you are being open-minded, you will have disarmed their hostilities, and progress toward a solution can be made. Remember to use body language that signals openness. When you have offered the first olive branch, that other person may also open up to you. Future dealings with that person will become easier once you have melted the initial iceberg with your discretion.

"The power of perspective is sufficient to halt the fiercest battle."
- Unknown

Step 3
Be Tactful

Tactfulness is the willingness to talk to people about their own interests; to weave elements of personal significance into a conversation that ignites the spark of pleasure in the mind of the other person. You should only talk to other people about their own interests after you have made an honest effort to find out what those interests are. Seek out commonalities between you and the other person and build on them.

For example, payday is always a safe, pleasurable subject. I used to work with this guy who was very difficult to engage in conversation and just not real friendly. However, he seemed to warm up to me every time the conversation topic had anything to do with money. Talking with this fellow about anything else seemed to lead to a dead end, so I began trying various conversation tactics, such as: "Only three days until payday – and payday is *my* favorite day. "

He began to open up, and when he would see me, he would say back, "Only two days 'til payday."

One day this back 'n forth banter turned into a pleasant conversation about benefits, merit increases and the stock market. As the months passed, he began to open up with me on other subjects and even laugh some. We eventually became good friends.

"Tact is the ability to describe others as they see themselves."
-Abraham Lincoln

Step 4
Be Patient

There is a very large payoff for being patient. Through exercising patience in my own business relationships, I have received immeasurable rewards. I could not have gotten where I am professionally without the cooperation of those whom I once believed to be difficult. Practicing patience with someone — especially someone you don't like — by listening intently before ever uttering a word, will gain that person's trust more quickly than anything else. The ability to listen without interrupting another person is a magnificent characteristic. But patience is more than just listening. Patience is giving someone your help and full attention when you really don't want to do it. It is taking the time to sit down with someone and explain something pleasantly until they understand it. The cooperation from others you will experience as the result of your effort in using patience will yield profound opportunity in your career, just as it did for me. I guarantee it.

"He that can have patience can have what he will."
-Benjamin Franklin

Step 5
Throttle Back Your Pride

Control your pride the same way you would drive a fine sports car. Sure, there are times to stomp on the gas and just let loose, but most of the time it is good to throttle back and baby the engine. *(If, that is, you enjoy the privilege of your driver's license).* The same is true in negotiations. Recognize the appropriate times to back off. Let the other person have the floor for a time. This can be especially difficult when you know the other person is wrong. Consider the pride of the other person. Consider the reward in sparing their feelings. The right time will always reveal itself for you to tactfully present your answer, without damaging anyone's ego. This is the key: hold back your own pride, even when you are in the right, and allow the other person to save face. You will win every time. If you maneuver through your professional dealings without injuring the dignity of other people, you will be paid back for your generosity in ways that you cannot possibly imagine.

"There is a healthful hardiness about real dignity that never dreads contact and communion with others however humble."
- Washington Irving

Step 6
Engage in Non-Random Acts of Kindness

When delivered with thought and precision, kindness is the most rapid way to eliminate tension between you and a coworker. Kindness may be delivered both directly and indirectly. Direct kindness, or generosity, may be displayed by going out of your way to make that other person's world just a little bit better. It is even okay if they don't realize that you did them a favor. Your time for recognition will come, and often at a point where it can do you twice as much good as "instant gratification" would have. How? By not demanding immediate recognition for your deeds, you are displaying that your efforts are genuine. While we are on this point, take note that it is, in fact, only genuine and authentic gestures of good will that can truly dissolve the tension that exists between coworkers.

"Indirect" kindness is a blanket gesture that would encompass many people, such as buying bagels or doughnuts for your whole group. Indirect kindness is giving someone a compliment behind his or her back. This is an encompassing action from which everyone benefits — including the person with whom you have been at odds.

Both direct and indirect acts of kindness require a strong amount of personal initiative on your part. Move your perspective beyond "Why should I?" and elevate yourself to a higher level. Be the person who engages in goodwill. It requires greater strength of character to be the person who will make the first move toward diffusing an unpleasant situation than it does to maintain hard feelings.

"Kindness is in our power, even when fondness is not."
-Samuel Johnson

Step 7
Avoid Debating Others' Global Beliefs

Have you ever noticed how some people at the office will put their own personal global beliefs up for debate? If you tune in, you can observe this happening all of the time. Dissention is created when one of the members of the team takes the bait and steps in to argue with the person who has inappropriately advertised their personal beliefs. Our advanced professional environment is no place for open discussions about political beliefs, religious beliefs or deep personal differences. If your co-workers are willing to play with fire and leave their personal beliefs open to disagreement, use tact and <u>steer clear</u>! In most cases your work pals just want your ear, and they don't want to be told anything different than what they currently believe. It will be incredibly advantageous for you to remember what you have read here, as this is the single most powerful way to completely avoid confrontation and argument.

"Many attempts to communicate are nullified by saying too much."
-Robert Greenleaf

Step 8
Use Your Mental Firewall

There are confrontations that are so intense, that the experience leaves your stomach wrenching for days and your head pulsating with the pressure of stress. That is, of course, only if you were not using the Mental Firewall. Remember that you own this new mental tool. It is your leverage with the provocative person. If the section in Chapter Two about your Mental Firewall is not clear, go back and re-read it. Make your Mental Firewall impenetrable by embedding it in your subconscious mind. By creating your Mental Firewall as a real, reactive force of your mind, you compound its effectiveness ten fold. It is a shield against people who attempt to upset you with their negative words and actions. Do not forget you possess a real, functional firewall.

"No one can make you feel inferior without your consent."
-Eleanor Roosevelt.

108

SUMMARY:
MAKING DIFFICULT PEOPLE YOUR ALLIES

Step 1: Think Accurately.

Step 2: See the World Through Their Eyes.

Step 3: Be Tactful.

Step 4: Be Patient.

Step 5: Throttle Back Your Pride.

Step 6: Engage in Non-Random Acts of Kindness.

Step 7: Avoid Debating Others' Global Beliefs.

Step 8: Use Your Mental Firewall.

One More Point...

Following the steps described in this chapter will allow you to get along effectively with anyone, even the most difficult people. Having said this, there is one more very important point I must relay to you before continuing. Always use your best judgment. There are jobs and companies where one or two people are difficult. This chapter was designed for handling those one or two people. There are also jobs and companies where everyone is difficult. Again, use your best judgment. If the people in your workplace are mentally abusive, it is time for an immediate change. If the people at your job are consistently negative, it is time to go. Don't fret if you do plan to leave your job. Later, in this book, I will help you devise a successful plan to search for a better job, a better company and ultimately a better career.

CHAPTER SEVEN

Eclipse Your Competition

It is exhilarating and frightening at the same time. There is no other feeling like it. That rush of emotion you experience, moments before you walk into your boss's office and announce your intent to leave the company. If you have ever done this, you know exactly what I am talking about. There I was, with my letter of resignation rolled up in my hand, standing outside Greg's office. I took a deep breath and collected my composure. I knocked on the door.

"Come in," a voice said.

I opened the door and encountered something completely unexpected. Not only was my boss in the office, but so was his boss, the Director of Information Technology. Suddenly, I felt my heart beating faster. What do I do? Do I come back later? A thousand thoughts must have raced through my head in the few seconds I paused. Despite the sudden rush of anxiety, I went inside. I told them both that I was leaving. I explained to them that because of the all of the layoffs that had taken place, I felt that I needed to find a more stable employment opportunity. They both sat quietly and listened to me outline my reasons. When I had finished, the Director spoke up. He said something that shocked me.

"You were never on the cut list, Chris. We'd like you to re-consider. You've done an outstanding job and you have surpassed all of our expectations. We have feedback on your performance from everyone with whom you have come in contact, and they said you go "above and beyond" every time."

I was beside myself. Although I had to turn them down, I simply could not believe that my name was never on the cut list, especially since everyone else on the IT team had years of seniority. Within those words that had been spoken to me, I found a precious jewel of knowledge. A jewel so valuable, that anyone who understands it and uses it will possess the power to truly secure their career. The jewel is this:

"You have surpassed all of our expectations."

After the initial shock, I had to find out why this one thing had provided me such a resilient *LayoffShield*. It seemed impossible that something so simple could be so powerful. I had to know. The Director of Information Technology already handed me the first clue. There is inherent power in surpassing others' expectations.

Your Precious Jewel: Surpassing Expectation

The habit of doing more than expected is a precious jewel because it is extremely rare. In fact, almost no one is doing it. The feeling of job dissatisfaction that millions of people feel today reveals itself as a low quality customer service experience commonplace in today's retail world. For working people caught in this trap, their true talent remains locked up, like a lion endlessly pacing back and forth in a cage. Their current job provides no escape for this talent, no gateway to the vast open plains, where their "lion" might engage its power. No, for these caged lions, surpassing expectation is unlikely because the labor of love simply does not exist. How do you do something extra and "go beyond" for your company when you don't enjoy what you do in the first place?

The other key reason that the practice of Surpassing Expectation has become such a precious jewel is that no one has time for it. The speed at which business is done has increased to an astounding level. This major boost in business speed, combined with the propagation of new business technologies, has changed the expectation of the American consumer. Instead of expecting personable, friendly service, consumer emphasis has shifted to the speed at which a product can be delivered. This is a model for today's businesses that can be seen everywhere. From pizza delivery to multi-million dollar e-commerce transactions, it's all about speed. Because the modern business focus is so concentrated on transaction momentum and the speedy delivery of goods, a necessary component for long-lasting success is lost.

This lost component is the ever-essential genuine human spirit of service. When the spirit of service dissolves from business, and is absent in customer transactions, there are no means through which a company may retain its customer loyalty other than boasting the lowest price for its products.

The Secret of Surpassing Expectation

What does it mean to consistently surpass the expectations of other people? It is actually comprised of a wide array of elements. First and foremost, you will want to engage in your work with a greater degree of pride. Distinguish yourself through your actions, by going a step further to serve someone when it is not necessary or required. Be friendly, polite and courteous with those whom you serve. Increase the scope of what you believe is possible through the work you do and to act on it. Extend the boundaries of your actions beyond the limitations of your job description into the realm of excellence. Go outside yourself and view the service experience through your customer's eyes. Practice generating a positive emotion in all those with whom you come into contact, simply by doing more than they expect of you. Surpassing expectation is setting someone else up to be successful. Engaging in this practice not only requires strong personal initiative, but it also calls for the courage to break out of your comfort zone and go beyond into the unknown. Practicing the business habit of Surpassing Expectation is highly valuable because it fulfills two fundamental human desires: *recognition* and *happiness.*

All of the Benefits That Will be Paid to You

Before diving into the all of the rewards you will receive by Surpassing Expectation, there is a higher benefit that must be recognized. This benefit is the warm glow of satisfaction you feel inside from knowing that you not only did your job well, but that you went out of your way to really help someone else. It is the personal gratification derived from the effort of doing more than the people around you. It is that sparkling exhilaration you experience when you know that you truly made a difference in someone else's day through the extraordinary service you have given to them.

The First Benefit:
The Stockpile of Favors

Imagine if everyone owed you a favor. How would that feel? What would it be like at your job if co-workers flawlessly covered your back when you were not there? What would it be like if you could get the cooperation you need from the key people in your company without going though any friction or confrontation? Imagine being able to easily "borrow" the expertise of another person for that critical part of your presentation. Wouldn't it be excellent if you were given "choice" assignments, doing the things in your job that you like best? This is not an imaginary list. Having a magnificent stockpile of favors from which you may draw is a highly powerful and very real benefit.

You receive this benefit by 'setting up' other people for success when they do not expect it. You actually "receive" in the long term by "giving" to people when they need your help. The result: You'll end up with a whole team of allies who are eager to do you a favor at the time you need it most.

The Second Benefit:
You Will Always Come Out On Top

If a sweet new job slot opened up inside your company, it would make sense that there might be some competition for it from within the ranks. If you are among those applying for this new position, you will want this second benefit. Build a strong reputation of consistently providing the extra effort, and when the time comes, you will be rewarded. The same thing applies if there are limited seats available for a special training event or travel opportunity. Make other people's jobs easier by lending a helping hand and you will reap the benefits of your actions.

The heart of this second benefit is untouchable by the layoff axe. Why? Through Surpassing Expectation, you are continuously sewing the seeds of kindness in others; and the evidence of this will be documented in your performance reviews, in kudo e-mails and in phone calls to your boss. Again, don't worry about getting instant gratification for your efforts. The payoff time will come. To quote Nike – "Just do it!"

Surpassing Expectation is the ultimate bridge builder. Through Surpassing Expectation, you will constantly construct new roads that will take you where it is want to go - specifically, through enhancing the work experience of the people you connect with everyday. Your eagerness to excel in areas where others are unwilling to go, will build your bridge to newfound opportunities.

The Third Benefit: Raises! Raises! Raises!

The real hallmark of Surpassing Expectation is that you can be singled out when it comes to raise-time. Here is common scenario you will often encounter in the professional arena. Managers are generally budgeted a specific amount of money to be used for annual merit increases for their group. This is usually a nice round number that is based on the premise that every member of the group will receive a three or four percent hike in income. I have experienced first hand that having a record of surpassing expectation has altered the standard merit increase percentage allotment, when I received an <u>eight percent hike</u> in annual pay.

Let's talk about bonuses for a moment. When a company exceeds *your* expectations with a bonus, it is an amazing feeling to have that unexpected extra money! For bonuses to come your way, you must first pave the road by putting in the extra effort to earn them. This goes without exception. I have seen situations where individuals have righteously assumed that they would be receiving a bonus, without so much as lifting a finger to do anything extra for their company. They just presumed that they deserved a bonus; and were actually upset when it did not happen for them. You don't want to be like those people. Instead, enlist the law of reciprocity as your ally and take the initiative.

Surpassing the expectations of the people in your company brings other kinds of raises your way as well. A raise may also come in the form of being offered a better position, which aligns more with your talents and makes your work more pleasant. Receiving a new job title can also be a way for your company to increase your salary beyond the prescribed yearly percentage. A raise can come in the form of having access to certain facilities and benefits that others may not have (for instance the company health club). Receiving training courses or qualifying for company paid college tuition should be considered a raise. Really, any action where a company invests more time and money in you is a raise.

Your company will invest more in you when you, FIRST, invest more in them! This key directive will unlock the treasure chest of bonuses, "perks" and a higher salary for you.

When Your Efforts Go Unnoticed or Unappreciated

Okay, so you could be thinking, I have tried all of this before and no one noticed. Perhaps some time ago, you went above and beyond, only to get knocked down because you inadvertently stepped on someone's toes when you were just trying to do them a favor. Maybe you did Surpass Expectation for some time and you saw someone who was doing less work get the reward. All of these things are possible. However, I would imagine that you are not the kind of person who lets other people and outside circumstances set the bar for you. If your employer truly does not notice your extra effort, then you have the prerogative to acquire a more considerate employer who will appreciate your services, recognize your extra effort and properly compensate you for it.

That is an extreme solution; however, your level of initiative and action depends on the severity of your circumstance. For instance, you may work for a great company, but your supervisor is, well, less than great. If that is the case, tap into your creative genius to score yourself another position inside your current company. It boils down to your personal happiness, your personal satisfaction and what you are willing to accept.

Extra effort and Surpassing Expectation comes from the true enjoyment of your work. This simply means that if you truly enjoy your work, going beyond and doing something extra does not actually seem "extra" to you because you enjoy doing it. The time you spend at work is a very large part of your life, and that time should be time well enjoyed. Do not let other people define how you feel in your job or career. That is completely in your charge.

Make Your Good Job a Great Job

If you are already working a job you love and you have no intention of jumping out the exit hatch, you can greatly enhance the quality of your daily experience at work. You begin through engaging your mind to seek more ways of providing a higher quality service experience for those with whom you work. How? You do this by knowing something about the jobs of the people around you and adjusting your actions to make their jobs easier. You take extra step in your job that removes a step from their job. The removal of the tiniest bit of work can make all the difference in someone else's world. If possible, knock something off of someone else's "to-do" list. You will be amazed at the positive feedback!

All too often we move and act only upon our own interpretation of an event, with our own needs in mind. The person who can shift their perspective on the fly and act with the benefit of another as their end goal in mind will have it all. They will have the *LayoffShield*. They will have friends and have fun at work. They will have the financial equivalent of the kindness they perpetuate. They will have it all.

Secure That Good Job

It is always a great idea to keep shining long after your hire date. What do I mean? I am not saying to arrogantly outshine everyone, or make a public display of always doing more than everyone else. No. There are better, and more subtle ways of showing that you are the best.

Let your good work speak for itself. Never brag that you went beyond the call of duty. The quality work you do will demonstrate that you care about the job you are doing, and that you do go above and beyond to do it. Be careful of the bragger's trap. It can be alluring to bathe in your own ego in front of others, but don't do it. Accept compliments gracefully and give credit to others when credit is due them.

The Golden Follow-Up

Lastly, secure your job with the "follow-up." This term is usually just thrown around in the sales arena, and is used as a means to generate more leads; however *LayoffShield* redefines the term and the action. Following up with someone exhibits genuine care or concern about a service you have done for them with the intention of improving your technique and bettering relations. Taking initiative to new heights and following-up with a person you have helped in the past is a gesture that will indeed eclipse your competition. This may be done through the use of 'Thank-you' cards or a friendly phone call to ensure that there are no problems or questions. If done with generosity and concern, your follow-up will weave itself into a tapestry of friendly and prosperous business relationships.

The Highest Form of Surpassing Expectation

This can be summed up in one word: *gratitude.* Gratitude alone has immense power. Used in business relationships, it builds bridges. It binds people to one another. It opens the door for repeat business. Effectively showing genuine gratitude for a favor or service someone may have done for you is one of the nicest things you can do for them. "Thank you, I appreciate that," when sincerely spoken, are the most powerful words in any professional career. Showing gratitude this way will work miracles in your career!

Nothing speaks like action. Acts of reciprocity can be more powerful than words. Next time you stop by Starbucks, pick up a drink for a pal who may have recently helped you out of a pinch. Your gift from "out of the blue" will be welcomed and remembered. Be creative in expressing your gratitude; use the personal likes of others as ideas for showing your genuine appreciation. Sure, it may cost five dollars here and there to do this, but the money is well spent and there is no better investment than the true expression of gratitude.

An important fundamental inside the principle of Surpassing Expectations is this: You've got to want to do it – or you're not really doing it. In other words, if you do something because you feel like you "have to" it robs the very spirit from the deed itself. Genuine intention is the driving force behind Surpassing Expectation.

SUMMARY:

THE BENEFITS OF SURPASSING EXPECTATION

The First Benefit: The Stockpile of Favors

The Second Benefit: Always Come Out on Top.

The Third Benefit: Raises! Raises! Raises!

The Boomerang Effect

Now it is time to move into action. Engage what you have learned in this chapter and experience first-hand all of the benefits by using: "The Boomerang Effect." Give it a throw and see what happens.

"No one ever attains very eminent success by simply doing what is required of him; it is the amount and excellence of what is over and above the required, that determines the greatness of ultimate distinction."
-Charles F. Adams

CHAPTER EIGHT

The Great Secret

This magnificent secret dates back almost two thousand years, and has been responsible for creating wealth, prosperity and happiness for those who embrace it. My own experience using this secret allowed me to achieve a degree-level position without a formal degree. The Great Secret is responsible for rocketing my salary higher than I'd ever dreamed, and it has drawn me closer to my own professional Zen of doing what I love and getting paid for it.

To understand the secret as a whole, you must first understand its parts. I will share the secret with you in the most empowering way possible, through a true story. This story led to my discovery of the secret and also represents one of the worst failures I've ever endured in my entire career — a failure so deep and powerful that it almost destroyed my future as a Network Engineer.

A Real-Life Success Story Using the Four Keys

PART TWO: The Greatest Defeat

I had come up with the perfect plan to protect myself from future layoffs. Accomplishing it would make me highly valuable to any employer. My plan was simple. I would take six specialized training courses as a means of gaining the skill and recognition to become a Certified Network Engineer with a Voice over IP specialization. The courses I had chosen were all on different technology sets and they complimented one another very well. Upon completion of the certification courses, I would wield an unstoppable skill set in the Telecom and Data Networking battlefield.

Unfortunately, the plan had big problems. Before ever getting in the classroom, I encountered two seemingly impassible barriers. The first big barrier was the 3K price tag of each certification course. I needed six classes. There was just no way that I could afford that. To make it even tougher, the second roadblock was the weekday schedule of all the training center classes, which conflicted with my working hours.

I was unwilling to accept those circumstances. Quitting was not an option. I kept asking myself how can I make my plan a reality? How? How? *How?* The human brain, being a highly powerful biological machine, found another option for me. I could become a self-study. I would be both the teacher and the student. I needed books. Not just books, but specialized guides and equipment that would be necessary to learn the material needed to pass the all six of the certification tests.

I decided to tackle the Cisco© CCNA© networking certification exam first. This exam by itself was a major endeavor, never-mind the five exams that would follow. To quickly familiarize you with this test, the CCNA© is a tremendously difficult computer based exam, rigorously testing the student's knowledge of Cisco© networking. This test will only grant you a passing grade if you score

85% or higher. To add some excitement, your score is revealed to you on the monitor just seconds after you finish the exam. Sounds like fun, yes?

I had to find help. I sought out people who were going the same route as I and teamed up with them. Working together, we formed an alliance and shared information with one another. With some diligent searching, I eventually found some actual networking hardware to practice what I was learning. I moved forward without a teacher, without a class and without formal training. My desire alone was going to have to be enough to pull this off.

Months of intense study passed by like a fast moving train. I converted the inside of my home into a giant whiteboard, complete with scribbled notes and study-guides plastered up on every wall. I dedicated every remaining minute of free time to absorbing the material. I recorded my own audio study guides on cassette so I could memorize facts while driving from place to place. This was the hardest I'd ever studied for anything in my life. I lived, ate and breathed nothing but CCNA©. A tremendous and vigilant effort, yes, but you won't believe what happened next.

I entered the testing center and laid down the test fee, one hundred and twenty five dollars. Next, I was shown into a private testing room that was complete with cameras. It was now test time. I was in the exam room for almost two hours, navigating my way through the test, intensely working question after question until I had reached the end. My score was revealed immediately: 83.7%

One question! I failed the certification test by just one question! I was floored. Five hundred hours of effort down the drain. I just could not believe it. When I saw my score, anger and disappointment saturated my mind like a damaged ship taking on water. The testing center Coordinator quietly gave me a printed copy of my examination report. I could not get over the bold print on the cover page: **FAIL.** As I was leaving, I tore the test report in half, crumpled the pieces into a little ball and tossed it in the back seat of my car.

"This is not worth it. I quit."

After working so long and hard, this was truly a monumental defeat and a bitter disappointment. I arrived home from the testing center with tears ready to burst from my eyes. The moment my wife saw my face, she knew that I had not passed.

"I am so sorry. I failed," I said as I handed her the crumpled ball of paper.

She un-crumpled both pieces of paper and laid them flat on the table. To my absolute surprise, she smiled.

"Look. You're so close. Go back and take it again."

Vanessa spoke those words with such spirit and enthusiasm, that she convinced me immediately. I examined my score report more closely, moving beyond the bold letters that graced the first page. It seemed that I had done exceptionally well in all but one of the categories. The section I bombed covered a technology called "switching." The intense frustration I felt earlier transformed into a hardened resolve and renewed determination. *Quitting was not the answer.*

I realized that by taking the exam and having experienced it once before, I was closer than ever to passing. I used the information I gathered from my score report to learn where I needed to sharpen my skill set. With full speed, I jumped right back in, studying the exact section of the test that had defeated me. I created an entire notebook containing the facts I needed to know about this specific category. With all of the tenacity I could summon, I attacked the subject, putting in long hours of study during the following week. At the end of the week, I re-entered the testing center and laid down another one hundred and twenty five dollars. Testing began . . .Two hours went by . . .

There is this *super*-intense moment at the end of every certification exam after answering the final question, and awaiting the exam results to be flashed on the screen. It is a five second slice of eternity. During those five seconds I felt my heart pounding in my chest like a sub-woofer. What an adrenaline rush! The screen flickered and then . . .**PASS**! I had done it! **PASS!**

A few weeks later, I received my first certificate in the mail. Although the CCNA© was a nice feather in my cap, it did not begin to compare with the first reward that I received as a direct result of my first "failure." This reward came to me disguised as a huge problem that occurred exactly six months after passing the test. I was now employed by a school district as a Network Technician.

"Everything is down."

It was a quiet lunchtime in the park. I was sitting on a bench overlooking a beautiful lake, eating a delicious sub sandwich. BEEP. BEEP. BEEP. My pager broke the silence. I read the text message as it scrolled across the tiny display. It was an urgent call for help. The district's largest high school was experiencing a major network failure. I packed up my half-eaten sandwich and rushed off in my car. After a short drive through downtown, I had made it. I burst through the doors of the front office to find a very frantic staff. Everyone's eyes locked on me. I will never forget that the school Principal had beads of sweat rolling off his forehead and an expression that could only be described as pure panic.

Everything had stopped. Three giant computer lab classes had come to an abrupt halt. The attendance system was completely down. The main office printers had stopped printing the semester report cards. Not a single e-mail message could be sent or received. The outage had also taken out the school's main web server. On the grand scale of network outages, this one ranked pretty far up there. Even though I had no idea what the problem was, I simply looked up at everyone and said, "I'll fix this."

I immediately went to work. Within forty minutes, I had tracked down and located the cause of the school's computer network meltdown. In the classroom of a distant wing of the school, a student had removed one of the wall jack plates and crossed the wires inside. By doing this, he created a very nasty kind of network failure, known as a loop. In a loop like this, every time a computer sends data through the network, the loop grows. In this case, when hundreds of computers send data, the loop grows so big that eventually it cascades throughout the entire building, over-loading the processors and memory of every network device, bringing things to a grinding halt.

Here's the kicker: The only reason that I was able to track down and isolate that particular network failure was because I had failed the CCNA© test the first time. Missing that one question put into motion a chain of events that caused me to go back and dedicate myself to thoroughly understanding "switching" technology. Had I not done that, I know for a fact there would have been no way that I would have been able to find and isolate that loop. The failure I experienced had revealed its first benefit to me. Reward number two was about to show itself.

The Principal was so ecstatic when the network was back up, that he called the Director of Information Services and proceeded to tell him how impressed and thankful the entire staff was that I had "saved" their school. The kudos just blew me away. A few days later, I received a classy gift from the office staff. Again, these events came about completely as a result of my CCNA© failure. But there's more. In the midst of some bad news to come, something even more incredible happened.

Two months passed. Huge budget cuts plagued the entire school district. Next came layoffs. No one was safe. Teachers, Administrative staff, Facilities Engineers and even Bus Drivers throughout the district were let go from their jobs. In fact, the school district's cutbacks were so large that they made the front page on both of the city's major newspapers. The layoffs overflowed and eventually spilled into our department. Along came reward number three. My job remained unscathed. Who was the person making the cut-lists for our department? You guessed it. That would be the same Director of Information Services who had received the call from the High School Principal about me. My "failure" had saved me again!

I believe, without a doubt, that my "Greatest Defeat" was actually the most beneficial event that could have ever happened to me. It is a fact that my failure on the test produced tangible benefits for me; benefits that both protected and upgraded my career as a Network Engineer. These marvelous events would never have taken place if I had decided to quit after failing the first exam. So it was not just the failure itself that had saved me; it was something more.

The Great Secret

The first historical account of the Great Secret is accredited to a young Roman citizen named Quintus Horatius Flaccus — Horace, for short. Horace had masterfully woven the words together that described the Great Secret for what it truly was. He wrote:

"Adversity has the effect of eliciting talents, which in prosperous circumstances would have lain dormant."

Down the generations the Great Secret passed. It surfaced once more, rendering aid to the greatest inventor in history, Thomas Alva Edison. Edison used the Great Secret in the creation of his most evolutional invention, and by using the secret he changed the world forever. Edison, with reference to his experiments preceding the perfection of the electric light, described the Great Secret in his own words:

"I am not discouraged, because every wrong attempt discarded is another step forward."

and

"I have not failed. I have found 10,000 ways that don't work."

Shortly thereafter, Andrew Carnegie used the Great Secret in his career to build the largest steel empire in the world. Before passing away in 1919, Mr. Carnegie entrusted the secret to a young journalist named Napoleon Hill. Embracing the Great Secret and taking it to an entirely new level, Napoleon Hill used the knowledge to organize the world's first philosophy of practical achievement. Dr. Hill accurately described the Great Secret in his own words, leaving absolutely no room for guesswork:

"Every adversity, every failure, carries with it the seed of an equal or greater benefit."

Possessing the Great Secret is to believe *all failures are actually opportunities,* regardless of whether or not those opportunities are immediately visible.

How does the secret really work? To answer this question, we need to explore the involuntary attitudes people take when confronted with defeat. These attitudes are our natural responses, our mental path of least resistance, so to speak. The first involuntary response we confront is anger. It is very easy to be angry when we lose or fail. Next comes negativity. It is very, very easy to be negative and see all of the bad things about a major adversity or failure. Next, is the desire to blame. It is very easy to place blame on other people. Have you ever seen anyone do this? Finally, there is the emotion of vengeance. To possess the desire for revenge against another is to make your primary focus negative, and that is detrimental to you, your career and your life.

It is, in fact, very easy to feel all of those things when we experience failure. When we focus on those negative emotions, a single small defeat can grow into a huge oak tree whose roots will carry harmful convictions deep into our minds. It happens so slowly that we don't notice. It's subtle, one little failure after another, over and over again, until one day we awake and realize that we have gotten so far off course that it seems impossible to ever get back. How many people have you seen caught in this trap? How many people do you know that are unhappy in their jobs with seemingly no hope – all because of how they view 'failure'.

Embrace the Great Secret and Use It

Challenge your natural responses to failure. Challenge your natural responses to defeat. Challenge your natural responses to loss. Challenge your natural responses to people who attempt to make you angry. Challenge your natural responses to the world. You were given the gift that only the human species has the privilege of ownership: the power of your *will*. Through use of your *will* you can master any defeat that you confront.

Attaching your focus to the negative aspect of a situation only magnifies and intensifies the problem, strangling your creative thinking. *Always* look for the inherent good that comes from any unfortunate circumstance in your career. Concentrate on creating opportunities that may not have existed prior to the failure or adversity.

I will not kid you — using your willpower to challenge the strong negative feelings that accompany a defeat is the harder road to go. However, if you choose to engage your willpower at the time of defeat and begin to look how that defeat can actually benefit you, you are separating yourself from the billions of other people on this planet who allow negative outside circumstances to rule their lives. This is the wisdom of the Great Secret.

The Great Secret has now been entrusted to you, just as it was entrusted to me and to others before me. You now have it within your power to make real changes in your career, in your income and ultimately in your life. I know without a doubt, when you absorb the knowledge in this chapter and make it into one of your most sacred convictions, you will experience an extreme elevation in your career like you have never experienced before!

"The value of liberty was thus enhanced in our estimation by the difficulty of its attainment, and the worth of characters appreciated by the trial of adversity."
-George Washington

CHAPTER NINE

The Swinging Axes in Corporate America

Knowing why layoffs happen empowers you to avoid them. The purpose of this chapter is to forge another coat of steel onto your *LayoffShield* by making you cognizant of the various layoff methodologies in Corporate America. My intent is to help you quicken your powers of observation and sharpen your sensitivity to layoff danger. You'll get an inside look at the key events and circumstances which underline the causative factors leading to corporate job slashing.

Fine tuning your mental alert system to be layoff savvy is rather easy. However, trusting and acting on that information can sometimes be more difficult. It takes a belief in yourself and in your convictions about what you predict will happen next. Combining your powerful intuition with the insight provided in this chapter will empower you with preemptive recognition of layoff symptoms and encourage you to take the appropriate action in advance of impending job cuts.

Layoffs are reflex actions. Corporations who engage in workforce reduction are reacting to a much larger event, (or series of events), herein referred to as "Prime Causes". We will examine each Prime Cause as well as the after effects and layoff methodologies used throughout corporate America. To provide you with maximum benefit, you will also be shown some very powerful layoff avoidance strategies.

#1 Prime Cause for layoffs in America: Corporate Expense Reduction

Across the United States, countless jobs vanish every year as the result of companies tightening their expenditures. This Prime Cause gains its momentum from a multitude of larger and more powerful events. The extreme pressure Wall Street applies to publicly held companies to report higher profits plays a lead role in Corporate Expense Reduction. Another high profile contributor to this Prime Cause is the amount of outstanding debt a company accrues. You've read about this scenario, I'm sure — corporations borrowing astronomical sums of money for hasty acquisitions, over-aggressive expansion or large real estate gambles that end up as liabilities after all of the dust settles.

There is a silent, yet equally detrimental force at work behind the scenes of U.S. Corporate Expense Reduction: world-wide competition. Over the last decade or so, the United States has experienced a steep increase in over-all global economic competition. This new competition is being driven by the world-wide expansion of advanced technologies combined with the emergence of highly skilled workers from nearly every corner of the globe, who are willing to work for significantly lower wages than their U.S. counterparts.

Finally, there is the perpetual fluctuation of consumer confidence that flows in and out like the tide. Consumer confidence may simply be described as the sum total of faith the American people have in the economy at any given time, and it is the largest barometer of our country's economic health. When confidence drops on a national level, consumer spending slows, business profits drop and Corporate Expense Reduction compensates with more job cuts.

What really drives key decisions when a company determines to reduce expenses by dismissing personnel, and how do they go about it?

The First After-Effect of Corporate Expense Reduction: Trim Layers of Management and Executive Staff

Inside every large corporate model, there are several layers of Management from the Executive level on down. It is here, in Management, where the job cutting begins. Managers are a prime target for layoffs for two reasons. First, their job function can be easily delegated to other Managers. Second, their rate of pay is generally higher than the average employee, which makes them more vulnerable to a layoff. A high Executive salary can become a liability when a company has fallen into the red. It makes sense; a company knows it does not really need fifteen Vice Presidents.

Yes, but who goes?

Weighing the value of a Manager during a time of pending job cuts raises several pertinent questions:

- What exactly are the Manager's specific duties?

- How critical are those duties to the continuation and success of the company?
- How easy is it to transition those duties to someone else?
- Who else in the company understands this Manager's duties?
- What is this Manager's track record and past performance?
- How valuable is this Manager's leadership to the company?

A crucial linchpin in the decision to layoff a Manager comes from the corporation's view of how a particular Manager's knowledge and level of operational understanding fit into the overall direction and growth plans of the company. The Manager who does not understand how the company's other departments function and interrelate may wind up being a very palatable layoff choice. Taking this insight with you, let's move toward defending ourselves.

Preemptive Actions you can take to avoid layoffs: (for Managers and Executives)

1) **Increase your knowledge.** Begin a quest to understand the systems, procedures, documentation and software programs that are part of other departments. See the larger picture in your company and think about how you can become a part of it. Increase your knowledge by getting involved with different aspects of your company's operations through offering to lend a helping hand. Begin to connect with other

people and go outside of your comfort zone. Ask questions. Use your Drive as a means to gain insight into the true substance of your company. Look for needs to be filled – and then act!

2) **Show your value.** The best thing you can do to protect your job is to show your value to the right people in your company. Identify who those people are. Tactfully show them how you have saved the company money, improved efficiency, accomplished corporate goals, and how your leadership has profited the company. One Manager I worked with had a brilliant strategy for showing the company her effectiveness. Her theory was this: Every Manager asks for budget dollars, but not every Manager shows how those dollars are working for the company after the fact. At the end of the year, she would present to a spread-sheet her Senior Management showing how each of the budgeted projects under her supervision were saving the company money. This initiative created value for herself and her entire department.

3) **Show your loyalty.** Practice your company's mission statement visibly. Vocalize your alignment with your company's direction and then act on it with genuine enthusiasm. Your team will adopt your attitude and pass it on to customers and employees alike. Also, when you, (or one of your team), is rewarded with an "atta-boy" e-mail or letter of appreciation, by all means, display it. Those precious letters will act as your shield, deflecting layoff arrows. Save every written compliment you receive and make certain to share

these letters with your Management. Contact your Human Resources Rep and ask her if your acknowledgement letters may be placed in your permanent HR file.

Use what you have learned here and combine it with your own ideas to communicate your value. Value can be communicated through accomplishment. Value can be communicated through other people's praise. Value can be communicated through your team's actions and performance. Show your company that it cannot live without you.

NOTE: *Use your best judgment when showing your company your value. Never damage or disparage anyone.*

The Second After-Effect of Corporate Expense Reduction: Offshore and Outsource Internal Departments

Offshoring seems to be running rampant! A number of the world's previously underdeveloped countries are now equipped with state-of-the-art corporate campuses, complete with modern fiber-optic data and telephone communication equipment. Inside these multi-million dollar campuses you will find highly educated technical workers, tax accountants, software developers, doctors, customer service representatives and thousands of other skilled individuals, all of whom provide specialized services to US corporations at a fraction of the normal operating cost.

Many American companies are taking advantage of this cost savings. Entire departments, once run in-house, are now being "farmed out" to foreign countries. This trend is growing at an alarming rate, stealing US jobs by the thousands every year. The numbers are staggering!

Outsourcing is also popular, as many US companies now specialize in providing "hosted services" at attractive prices. While these solutions seem distasteful to you and I, it is important to realize that both offshoring and outsourcing are very alluring to CFO's who must reduce operating costs while maintaining productivity.

With the explosive growth of these trends, you must act prudently to avoid losing your job to an entire overseas population who is eagerly awaiting your paycheck. You might ask, "How can I avoid being laid-off if my whole department is offshored?" That is a great question. Here are the answers.

Preemptive Actions you can take to avoid layoffs caused by Outsourcing and Offshoring:

1) **Build long-term recognition with your employer.** No one else can do what you do. A great method of building long-term recognition with your employer is accomplished by using your expertise and knowledge to help solve big problems. It is good to be known as the "only person who knows how to do that." Seek problems that need resolution *and act.* Do not be afraid to offer potential solutions to other people's problems. When the upper Management team connects your name with being a *problem solver*, you will have strengthened your *LayoffShield* significantly.

2) **Connect! Connect! Connect!** A huge part of building long term recognition with your

employer means connecting with as many people within your company as you can. Get your name out there! Make some new friends. Accept assignments where you will be in contact with other teams within your company. Make it a point to introduce yourself to people when you can. Be friendly! Get involved in as many functional areas as you can, through your interaction, you will no doubt build new relationships.

3) **Use your untapped talent!** Everyone one us possess untapped resources and talents that are part of our inner makeup. Getting out of your comfort zone and demonstrating your ability in areas other than your own will ensure longevity with your employer. Think of it like this: You want to be able to do more for your company than your overseas counterpart. When you are recognized as someone whose capability and willingness to help goes far beyond their job description, you will be given a hand up instead of a pink slip!

4) **Act in advance.** The fourth strategy for countering an offshoring/outsourcing scenario is to anticipate it and act in advance. Major outsourcing decisions by companies are not made in a day. In fact, it's just the opposite. Big decisions are planned far in advance. Outsourcing is a carefully calculated maneuver that is usually preceded by a number of subtle warning signs.

Don't ignore the sudden appearance of outside consultants at your office. Be aware of any secret meetings in upper Management and question the seemingly harmless requests to complete informational forms that describe your job parameters and professional skill level. Refer to Chapter Three, "The Ability to Anticipate Intelligently". The Four Keys that are referenced in that Chapter will help you detect a big outsourcing move by your company before it actually happens.

The Third After-Effect of Corporate Expense Reduction: Across-the-Board Layoffs

When a human body is exposed to extreme cold temperatures for an extended period of time, it begins shutting down the blood flow to the unnecessary organs to minimize heat loss. Next, the body begins to slow its metabolism, requiring less energy to function and expending less oxygen in order to stay alive as long as it possibly can.

Across-the-Board Layoffs are the result of a company doing exactly the same thing. Every single department is analyzed for its overall necessity to corporate survival. If the department is not deemed vital, it is disbanded and all the employees in that department are let go. When the depth of a company's financial trouble is nearing critical mass, it is no office secret, especially if that company is publicly owned.

Preemptive Actions you can take to avoid "Across-the-Board" Layoffs

1) **Voice your Commitment.** In most cases, Across-the-Board Layoffs happen pretty late in the game, with numerous indications preceding the actual layoff event. At this point you would already

know if your company was in trouble. If you are willing to stay with your company through its darkest hour, then you need to communicate your sincere commitment to anyone in Management who will give you their ear. Loyalty is valuable to a company that is desperate to survive, despite the ominous circumstances.

2) **Do not hold back any action**. During times of heavy financial pressure, your company is actually looking for innovative solutions to some very hard problems. Be the person who comes up with answers. Deviate from your regular agenda and brainstorm with others to create practical ideas to help your company. Increase your contacts within the company as a means to share your loyalty with those who are not poisoned by negative press and hearsay. Gather the troops and act in any way you can to help your company. Be bold with your actions. Now is not the time to hold back. Do not be afraid to approach the Executive level members of your company and share your ideas and enthusiasm. Lastly, the hallmark of true company loyalty is being able to represent your company to the outside world with the same passion and conviction you would if it were not in trouble.

#2 Prime Cause for Layoffs in America: Business Model Changes

The rate of change in business in the 21st century is simply astounding. Technology and high speed communications have completely reshaped the business world. The amount of technology we possess as a global society is mind-bending. More incredible than the technology itself, is the rate at which it is growing.

Companies are consistently using technology as the means for improving operations in order to minimize their expenditures. Technology drives corporate efficiency, employee accountability and consumer demand. These three factors are causative influences in Business Model Changes, the second Prime Cause for Layoffs in America. There are two important facts to remember about Business Model Changes:

1) If a business method, operational implementation, or legacy technology can be replaced by a more efficient (cost-saving) technology, it will be.

2) Consumer demand drives Business Model Changes.

The First After-Effect of Business Model Changes:
Employees working with legacy technologies are the first to be let go.

In 2005, 10,000 employees at the Kodak Company were let go from their jobs because Kodak closed several of its film manufacturing plants. This action was sparked by the increased demand for digital products and a lack of demand for traditional film cameras by the consumer. This is one of hundreds of cases where new technology changed both consumer desire and corporate operations. It is important for you to be able to recognize these large scale trends and calculate how your job may be affected.

Preemptive Actions you can take to avoid Layoffs caused by legacy technology abandonment

1) **Use your existing knowledge as a springboard.**
   Instead of allowing your background in a legacy
   technology to be a hindrance, use your specialty
   and expertise as a foundation for future learning.
   Although fundamental differences may exist,
   many newer technologies must conform to same
   set of rules as their predecessors. For example, even
   though digital cameras use electronic medium to
   store images, the new camera design still requires
   basic features such as a lens, shutter, light-proof
   casing, aperture, etc.

Inventory your existing knowledge. Compare your
current knowledge with what you understand about the
new technology and then begin to work on filling in
the gaps. For example, if I worked for Kodak designing
traditional cameras, I would take it upon myself to learn
the fundamentals of digital imagery. I would then find
out how these traditional camera components integrate
with the digital medium. Or, if my position at Kodak
centered on chemical film development, I would now
focus my learning efforts toward understanding both laser
and ink jet printer technology. I would make known my
intention to help Kodak with its goal of perfecting the
printed output of the digital image.

2) **Take the initiative.** As soon as you detect the
   slightest hint of possible change, put your mind

into overdrive to learn all you can about it. Take the initiative to become involved and learn what is new, rather than waiting for your company to train you. For instance, an Automotive Technician working in the service department of a dealership should seek opportunities to acquire technical training that would certify him to service the newly emerging hybrid engines. First, he would look inside the company for the training he desires. If he hears the same old song and dance from his boss, "We don't have the budget this year to send you to training; maybe next year.", that response would be the signal for the Technician to move forward on his own initiative. When he does proceed to get the training on his own, two great things will happen. First, he increases the future demand for his services throughout his industry. Second, he is not at all dependant upon the whims of a single employer, (or sometimes a single person), for the future success of his career.

Regardless of what you do for a living, whether you are a traditional camera specialist or an automotive technician, if you use the first Key from Chapter Three of this book, "A Burning Curiosity for your Profession," you will not be caught off-guard by industry changes in your field.

3) **Always be seeking opportunities to use your skill set.** Seek opportunities both within and outside your company. Your professional

background has true value. *Never believe otherwise.* You never know the endless opportunities that await you unless you are actively looking for them. Opportunities are often disguised as undesirable tasks, so be sure to keep your mind open to every possibility and direction that is available to you.

The Second After-Effect of Business Model Changes: Layoffs caused by corporate restructuring

Business model changes reflect more than just technology. Major changes often occur as a result of corporate growth and maturity, (or sometimes because of costly mistakes). Companies normally grow and mature through bringing about small changes over time. These small shifts and changes can be attempts by companies to gain a particular advantage in their business arena.

Just to give you an idea, you might see the changes materialize if your company is centralizing key operations and personnel to a single office. Another change could be combining business functions that overlap for efficiency's sake. Or, a company could be moving away from multiple software platforms, when one will do the job. Unfortunately, changes such as these often do bring about significant layoff events.

Preemptive Actions you can take to avoid Layoffs caused by Corporate Restructuring

1) **Be alert and don't be afraid to act.** Here is where it really pays to be tuned into the direction of your company. The series of smaller changes that can

lead layoffs are usually part of a larger pattern that is recognizable to someone who has their finger on the company's pulse. Seek information and facts about your company as a means to identify a pattern that indicates a distinct business direction. For instance, see if your company is continuously marketing certain product lines more heavily than others. Look at recent acquisitions as a means to indicate business directions. There is a reason that your company purchased the smaller company. Find out what it is. Look where the industry is headed as a whole and if your company is aligned with that direction. Once you discover your company's direction, visualize how you and your department fit into the overall scheme. Ask yourself, "Is my job function being centralized?" Is my job obsolete? How will my skill set and job function produce for my company in a year or two from now?

Just as a reminder, the questions listed in Chapter Three, "The Ability to Anticipate Intelligently," are great to start you on an information search and help you gauge your vulnerability. Once you've assessed that you may be vulnerable to a coming layoff, take action immediately. Do not hesitate, or reverse your decision, once you have decided to act.

2) **Get in on the action.** When uprooting and centralizing take place in a company, there will be masses of people who complain, people who engage in negative gossip and people who bathe

in self-sympathy. Instead of joining that crowd, be the person who steps up and wants to get in on the action. Become a part of your company's plan. If your home life and family responsibilities permit, offer your services to an out-of state branch of your company. Go to your company's HR web site and look for job postings. Reach out and ask questions; consider new possibilities and find out as much as you can about what, exactly, your company is doing. Be on constant lookout for ways to derive benefits from the changes that are facing you.

The Third After-Effect of Business Model Changes: Employee accountability & productivity tracking technology causes Layoffs

Thanks to recent advances in several different areas of technology, the productivity of any employee can now be calculated down to the minute. Technologies such as mobile phone GPS, On-star vehicle tracking, computer desktop monitoring software, card access keys, call-tracking software, website trackers and various other technical-based tracking methodologies permit companies to obtain very detailed reports on the efficiency levels of every employee. The company sees one thing and one thing only: Low efficiency equals loss of dollars.

Preemptive Actions you can take to avoid Layoffs caused by Employee Activity Tracking

1) **Exceed the standards**. Companies use activity accountability technologies as "slacker-trackers", to ensure that employees are doing their jobs. Although some employees might view micro-accountability as an invasion of privacy and fear a "Big Brother" scenario, a fantastic opportunity actually exists for those who choose to play by these rules. Accountability practices are often based on average performance standards, computer generated models and other "low-bar" style rules. The fact that your performance is being measured is actually a very good thing. It gives upper management visibility into the fact that you exceed standards and expectations. You stand out on their graphs, charts and reports. Over time, the fact that you stand out above the crowd will pave the way for advancement and keep you off the cut list.

2) **Get on a different team.** If your team is failing and you are being measured by a group's performance, it is time to find a different ship in the fleet on which to serve. If not, you are likely to go down with your current crew and ship. Be constantly aware of the over-all performance of your team as well as your team's necessity to the company. As always, do not hesitate to act when your gut feeling tells you that you are in the wrong place.

Prime Cause #3 for Layoffs in America: Corporate Mergers, Takeovers and Restructuring

Countless jobs are lost through corporate mergers. To best protect yourself from being laid off, you should have a clear understanding of what actually happens when a large corporation absorbs a smaller corporation. The smaller corporation's core values are replaced with new ideals, new practices and new ways of doing things. It is no longer the same company at all. Old rules do not apply. Old accomplishments no longer matter. The seniority, reputation, and status of all the "absorbed" employees are now blank slates. This is a very hard reality for some to swallow, especially those who have spent years building their own careers within their company. Accepting this unpleasant truth is necessary if you are to defend your position.

The First After-Effect of Mergers: Eliminate redundant departments and personnel

The merger has already cost the parent corporation millions of dollars; therefore, upon completion of the merger, the first order of business is to avoid paying salaries to duplicate departments when one can do the job. In some cases, the duplicate departments may have been pre-identified at an earlier date, permitting the layoff axe to swing the same day the merger papers are signed. The list of redundant departments and personnel can range from the employees at the top executive level all the way to the night-time janitorial crew.

Permit no gaps in your income.

Build and execute your own pre-merger strategy. Because the cut-lists are drafted before a merger is complete, you must also act beforehand. The truth is, you don't know if the new company is going to keep you or not. If you are anticipating a merger or buy-out, it is best to design your own plan concerning your job, rather than doing nothing and hoping everything works out when the dust settles. Begin to act as soon as you get wind of a possible merger. Map out some different companies you would like to work for. Get your resumé tuned up and get it posted. Surf the net and zero in on attractive-looking jobs. Do not be afraid to act and decide your own path.

NOTE: *If you are somewhat unsure if your company is a target for a buy-out, please refer to the Corporate Acquisitions and Mergers Section in Chapter Three. The questions listed in that section will assist you in your research.*

The Second After-Effect of Mergers: Weed Out and trim away specific members of the workforce

One of the goals of a larger company, when acquiring a smaller company, is to keep operations running smoothly. The company accomplishes this goal through eliminating all non-team players and indoctrinating the rest of the new employees with its practices, philosophies and values. One common practice is appointing an Executive or Manager from the new company as the lead of a team in the acquired company. That Executive or Manager is then given the assignment to weed out people. The weeding process involves removing individuals who are close-minded toward new company practices or who are hostile about the changes that are taking place. Any person who demonstrates an unwillingness to accept the new company platform and clings to the "old-way" will be laid off. The new company knows without a doubt that negative-minded employees are detrimental to its success and will act to eliminate them.

Preemptive Actions you can take to avoid Layoffs caused by the Weeding Out process

1) **Be a part of the new ship and crew.** To ensure your continuance and lock in your place with the new company, your key strategy must be *genuine cooperation.* Express enthusiasm through your willingness to help your new co-workers and Managers acclimate. Remember the names of all of the new people now working with you. Use your initiative and see where others need help. Be a communication bridge between the two groups to help get things moving. Above all, demonstrate your loyalty to your new employer through making it a point to learn about the new company, who the leaders are and their business values.

2) **Turn negative into positive.** If you overhear co-workers in a conversation bashing the new company, tactfully offer a positive slant. Be a positive influence. Do not be afraid to voice an upbeat opinion in meetings, lunches and at the water-cooler. Your goal should be to gain a reputation within the new company as a "positive

person." There is no doubt that having a true positive mental attitude adds to the overall effectiveness of your *LayoffShield*.

3) **Show your value all over again.** Demonstrating your value as an employee requires a diligent effort, especially when a new company has come in and taken charge. Offer to solve problems that others are unwilling to solve. Step forward when Management calls for volunteers. Do not be afraid to share your expertise and background with other people when the time is appropriate. Display your certifications, awards and certificates in your workspace. Share your "kudos" e-mails and letters with your new Manager.

The Third After-Effect of Mergers: The "Learn and Burn"

This somewhat questionable layoff methodology dwells in a very remote corner of the business ethics universe, and unfortunately, it occurs frequently enough to warrant a place in this book. If you have not guessed, the "Learn and Burn" occurs after one company has bought out another company and the larger company keeps the staff of the acquired company onboard solely for the purpose of learning how things work. Once the learning process is complete and the knowledge has been attained, the employees from the acquired company are laid off.

The Learn and Burn occurs in departments where the job functions and duties are somewhat intricate and are not easily understood. For example, a company's I.S. (Information Services) department is highly susceptible because of their involvement in technology. Employees from this department cannot be dismissed on day one of a new merger because they are crucial to sustaining communications and operations. However, once the details of technology systems have been revealed to the parent company, the original employees become prime layoff targets. You get the picture, I am sure.

Preemptive Actions you can take to avoid Layoffs caused the "Learn and Burn"

1) **Watch for mirroring. Beat them to the punch.** A good sign that you are being eyed for a Learn and Burn is if you are asked to have a new employee mirror you. The purpose of the "mirror" is for this person to learn your duties and everything they possibly can about the systems you manage. The "mirror" will ask you for documentation, passwords and other key information. To uncover the truth about whether or not you actually are a valuable member of the new team, ask yourself if the person mirroring you is sharing as much real information with you as you are sharing with them. If the new company is setting you up for Learn and Burn, you will most likely be kept out of the loop about new plans and projects. Lastly, beat them to the punch. Don't wait passively. When in doubt, act immediately. Get your resumé out on the web and begin the hunt.

2) **Be a better employee than the person who is mirroring you.** So, you are not willing to let go of your job that easily, eh? Great. If you truly do know your job better than anyone possibly could, look for opportunities to communicate this fact

to the decision makers. You must "show up" the person who is lined up for your job slot. Do what your competition is unwilling to do. Beat your "mirror" to the punch when solving problems. Show you are smarter, faster and a better overall choice for the job slot. Go above and beyond expectation to keep your work a step above your counterpart's efforts. Connect with people in the new company and make friends. Identify the decision-makers and make connections with them. Show them that you are a great employee and that you are completely loyal.

NOTE: *Due to the variety and number of topics covered in this chapter, rather than summarize the information, I thought that you, the reader, would derive maximum benefit through simply reviewing the strategies set forth.*

Use your Layoff Shield!

The inherent force that *is* the armor of your *Layoff Shield* is action. You have the knowledge. Take what you have learned in this chapter and use it to forge a *Layoff Shield* that is completely invulnerable to <u>all outside influences</u>! Never underestimate yourself! The electromotive force within you - your ability to take action - is incalculably powerful! This is an incredible fact which merits your most profound consideration.

"Twenty years from now you will be more disappointed by the things you didn't do than by the ones you did do. So throw off the bowlines. Sail away from the safe harbor. Catch the trade winds in your sails. Explore. Dream. Discover."
-Mark Twain

CHAPTER TEN

Do What You Love and Get Paid

Why is it that so few people seem to reach that career they really love? Through my own passionate study of career enhancement philosophy, I have found that there are two fundamental reasons for the high rate of job dissatisfaction that dominates America. The first reason is the complete lack of belief that such a thing is actually possible. *Belief is everything.* The second reason that most people get caught in the web of job misery is that they inadvertently choose careers where their real talents and abilities are never truly let of out the cage. Our time here is far too valuable to be spending sixty percent of our waking hours at a job that makes us feel miserable. Wouldn't you agree?

If you permit me, I will raise the curtains and reveal to you that a career of enjoyment and wealth is well within your grasp. This is a fact and is worth repeating. *A career of enjoyment and wealth is well within your ability of attainment.* It is possible regardless of whether or not you hold a degree. It is possible regardless of who you are, where you come from or how much money you have. None of that matters. I only ask that you suspend any doubt that exists in your mind, suspend any beliefs you may have and open your mind to the possibility of possibilities. It is the greatest favor you will ever do for yourself. Imagine never again dreading going to work. Instead, you look forward to it. Sound impossible? It's not.

The reality of doing what you love and getting paid for it takes the form of a very powerful plan, a plan whose elements are backed by a combination of proven success principles. Please allow me to present . . .

The Science of a Successful Plan

If you've ever felt like you were meant for something greater, or you have an incredible idea that you would like to develop, or you just wanted to do something different than what you are doing now, but you just did not know how to do it, the Science of a Successful Plan is for you. Simply put, this plan will show you how to make your own dream come true. The framework of this plan is made up of eight distinct elements, all of which are equally important to your success. Knowing this, as you read this chapter, please keep in mind that it is absolutely necessary to use all eight of the elements (rather than picking out the parts you like and only doing those). Okay, no more build up. Let's get started immediately.

Element #1:
Create Your Powerful Vision

When you are beginning to construct the framework of your own career plan, remember that you hold the freedom to secure both financial abundance and economical security through your talents. Do not let career-inhibiting convictions govern the degree to which you set your sights. Aim high, because it is *you* who decides what you can and cannot do. There can be no stronger truth. Reach out and choose the job or career you love, *and be definite about it.* When you have reached a decision concerning your career of prosperity and enjoyment, the crucial first step in making that choice come true is being able to actually imagine it.

When you unroll the blueprints of your plan onto the drafting table in your mind, take note that the *practicality* of your plan's outcome is not as important as the *certainty* of your plan's outcome. Remember that. The "how" comes later. The "what" is far more crucial. Knowing this, be very precise about what you are going after and jam the gearshift of ambition into overdrive and stomp on the throttle of your imagination.

The use of your creative thought is a multi-dimensional process. When you imagine, you have the use of your five senses at your disposal. Your imagination houses far more power and special effects capabilities than George Lucas' private Home Theater, so the sky is the limit. Create the scene on your mind's stage. See the outcome of your plan. See yourself already doing what you love. Experience yourself being paid for it. Touch the money you will be making. Hear the sounds around you in your new job. Smell the gourmet coffee at your new office. Whatever you envision, emotionalize the experience of your plan's outcome in your mind. This can be a lot of fun. Just remember to be exact with what you are imagining and be repetitive. How often should you visualize yourself in your ideal scene? As often as humanly possible. Why, you may ask?

When you place repetitive effort toward multi-dimensional creative thought and visioning, you are not only exercising command over your most powerful asset, but, more importantly, you are actually telling both halves of your mind that what you are imagining is indeed possible. This is the key. When the sub-conscious mind begins to view the attainment of your objective as a *real* possibility, it immediately goes to work on *how* to achieve that objective. Your sub-conscious will then begin to feed you ideas and solutions to the problems you face concerning your plan. It's nothing short of amazing. The method of repetitive creative visioning, in my eyes, is one of the most effective ways of tapping the incredible human potential that resides within us.

Element #2:
Build a Concrete Motive

Your motive is the heart of your plan. It is what breathes life into your plan and keeps it moving forward when the entire world seems to be against you. Motive is one of the most powerful forces that you and I as human beings can harness and command.

Your motive needs to be rooted deep inside you, as it is part of who you are. Your motive will show itself in the way you walk and it will reflect itself in the tone of your voice when you speak. It will reveal itself as enthusiasm in all that you do. The best thing about possessing a motive is that it increases your willpower to extraordinary levels. Next, motive combines willpower with imagination to create a very high level of innovative thought that is capable of surmounting the difficult obstacles that accompany any significant plan of action. Let's talk more about this second element of a Concrete Motive. How do you actually go about making a motive concrete?

First, you must be true to yourself and take the time to reach deep inside yourself to really find out what your motives of success are. For a motive to be concrete, it must be something in which you truly believe. It could be something you really, really, really want, even if it is as simple as not letting a corporation control your destiny. That one thought alone can be very powerful. In my case, it was my wife and my son that provided me with my concrete motive. They gave me the motive to aim for something way beyond anything I had ever achieved. Through focusing on them as my motive, it became permanent inside me. It was this force that propelled me toward my desires without the option of retreat.

Second, make it a point to feed and strengthen your motive everyday. Inject your strongest emotions into your motive and give it your continuous thought attention. Use motive-reminders, such as *the Environment of Greatness* to help you to maintain your focus on your motive. Allow your motive to dominate your thoughts and flow through your veins. Let it grow and thrive inside you.

When your motive has completely saturated you to the brink of obsession; it is then concrete. It is at this point that your motive will never allow you to shift your focus away from what you truly desire. It will never let you compromise for anything less than what you have set your sights on. It will not allow other people to deter you in any way, as their negative comments will be as ineffective as water balloons against a Loomis Fargo armored truck. Lastly, remember that at the heart of any successful plan lies motive, so use your motive to move forward with certainty and courage in your pursuit.

Element #3:
Believe In Yourself

Your thoughts are the rivers that fill the ocean of your mind with confidence. Confidence is one of the most important elements in the Science of a Successful Plan. Why? It's simple. Confidence backs action. Without confidence, there would be no action. Confidence in your own abilities to do the things necessary to carry out your plan is absolutely essential. This level of conviction in yourself is not built from comparing yourself to other people, (which most of us do). Instead, it is built from the inside out. Confidence is built through the recognition of your own true power, a power that is so great, that it gives you the capacity to command your life as you see fit.

Confidence begins with an accurate understanding and definition of confidence itself. Confidence is a feeling, an emotional state that you produce and control. That's right, *you* command it. Confidence is a mental attitude through which you continually focus your thoughts upon the belief in yourself and belief in your abilities. Confidence comes through completely clearing your mind of doubt and disbelief, despite whatever outside circumstance exists. Even a few seconds of this magnificent style of thinking is enough to produce real action. Action, made in an effort toward the attainment of your plan, re-fuels the confidence in yourself. The perpetual relationship between confidence and action is inseparable, and it is the engine that will provide unlimited power for the attainment of your plan.

The traditional paradigm that society gives us about having an ego is so off target. It is necessary to have an ego where your belief in yourself and your abilities to break the barriers of high achievement are concerned. It is absolutely necessary to have the full conviction in your own abilities to get the very best of what life has to offer. Putting real effort into the cultivation of confidence and belief will pay out large rewards and eventually fill your professional world with pride and accomplishment.

Okay, but how do you train your mind to think at this level?

Find your Confidence Triggers. As human beings, each one of us is highly unique; therefore our confidence triggers are unique. Confidence triggers are the internal and external stimuli that invoke the powerful emotion of confidence. For some people, the triggers are auditory. Music is a huge confidence trigger, and its power is unmatched in its ability to completely change a person's emotional state. For others, a confidence trigger may be remembering a powerful event in their life and drawing from it. Some people are moved to confidence by visual triggers, such as the portrait of a personal hero. Take the time to discover your own personal confidence triggers.

Seek the evidence of greatness inside you. To have a stronger and more defined sense of confidence, begin by giving your focus and attention to all of the things you value within yourself. These things might be qualities that have not yet had the privilege of your everyday awareness and continued attention. There exists an entire stockpile of these kinds of things inside you. Like what? Your abilities, talents, accomplishments and victories are all elements that warrant your thought awareness. It does not stop there. Your "gifts", as I like to call them, can range all the way from your specialized skills to the power of your personality to create a smile on the face of another.

Seek out all of the things you value about yourself and make the time to become consciously aware of your great qualities.

Find physical evidence of confidence. There also exists physical evidence of these great qualities you possess. Go on a hunt and search through your attic and dig out your ribbons, certificates and trophies going as far back as you can. Collect all of the memorabilia of your past victories and go through and take the time to look at each item. Remember how you felt when you received each award. Find new frames for your certificates to replace the old cracked ones. If you have trophies that have been forgotten, polish them and make a place for them in your home. Make them part of your Environment of Greatness. All of the awards and merits you have ever received will act as constant fuel for a consciousness of confidence. You are great. There is proof. Find it and use it.

Don't think you can, *know* you can. In the movie, *The Matrix,* there was a powerful quotation, spoken by the character of Morpheus, who said to his student, Neo, "*Don't think you can, know you can.*" I use this as a reference simply because it so perfectly states the key to the entire concept. It is this level of conviction that I want you to experience after reading this book and putting the ideas within it into action in your life.

It all can be summed up with one word: *belief.* It is ultimate belief in yourself that unlocks the otherwise dormant powerful abilities that are inside you now. This belief is to possess the willpower to "know," without relying on the logical thought process of knowing how. You already possess the willpower to do this; all you need to do is use it.

Lastly, become a student of confidence. If your appetite for knowledge exceeds the slice of pie that has been served to you here, that is good. I encourage you to become a student of confidence. Make the attainment of self-confidence one of your must-have targets. There are shelves and shelves of books and self-empowerment programs out there on this concept. Make the building of confidence a ritual that you perform day in and day out, never stopping.

Element #4: Synchronize Your Plan's Ultimate Outcome Between Both Halves of Your Mind

Once you have zeroed in on exactly what it is you intend to acquire through the means of working your plan, the outcome must be recognized and accepted as extremely positive by both halves of your mind. In other words, your entire mind must be completely synchronized to the outcome of your plan and all of the effects it will have on your life. If any part of your plan is regarded as negative by your deeper beliefs, your plan will never run its course. It needs the tremendous power of your subconscious mind to back it. I'll explain.

Often, what looks good to the conscious section of the mind may not be all that attractive to its power-producing counterpart, the subconscious. As an example, suppose that that outcome of your plan involves the changing of jobs. That is great. The new job means higher pay, an opportunity to advance and, to top it off, a much better benefit package. All seems great. At a glance, it seems we have covered all the meanings that achieving a new job could have. Or have we?

169

A further look inside must be taken to be certain. Accepting a new position would also mean getting out of your comfort zone. This is huge for some people. Years and years doing the same job and being completely comfortable in a position can make a change difficult. A new job would also mean leaving people with whom you have made strong connections and friendships. These two things could act as a gigantic anchor that has one hook deeply wedged in the earth, ultimately chaining you down and keeping you from your real desire.

Avoid "spinning your wheels."

I must emphasize again importance of having the entire outcome of your plan completely synchronized throughout your entire mind. Action without absolute synchronicity is simply "spinning your wheels" because your entire mind is not really on board with what you are doing. Knowing this, be sure you are fully cognizant of all the effects the outcome of your plan has on you, your loved ones and your life.

To further illustrate the importance of completely understanding the effects of a non-synchronized outcome, I'll give you a good example, using my own plan. The outcome of my plan involved the attainment of a significant amount of money. Everything seemed okay at first, but after a close examination of my own convictions about money (that I'd absorbed through social heredity), I found that deep inside, I felt that having a lot of money was not a good thing.

What could possibly be bad about money?

I used to believe that "rich" people were conceited snobs who nobody liked. That is the way they were drawn in cartoons and portrayed in TV when I was growing up. I thought all rich people were like Mr. Howell on *Gilligan's Island*. I also felt that possessing any kind of wealth at all made me less spiritual. To me, there was no such thing as a friendly, kind or spiritual rich person. I bought into the whole "money is the root of all evil" lie. These beliefs I had as a youngster solidified into hard-core facts. When Friday's paycheck came, I usually had it spent by Sunday. As you can guess, my subconscious made sure that I never mounted any meaningful effort toward financial prosperity. I always made just enough money to survive. I was chained down by my own mind, until . . .

I took command over my belief system.

Through an extensive study of men and women who led extraordinary lives, I discovered evidence that proved the exact opposite of what I previously believed about money. As a result, I adopted a new belief system that allows me to hold an abundance of money in my life, comfortably balanced with strong spirituality. I know that money is a thing; it is a lifeless piece of paper. It is the holder, the owner of money, who chooses the direction and the lifestyle. I believe that having an abundance of money does not make a person materialistic or snobbish; instead, ample money empowers the individual to offer help to others on a larger scale and allows its holder to enjoy many of the fun adventures that life has to offer.

Be the Architect of your own beliefs and synchronize your mind.

Make sure that you do not hold any deep-rooted negative thoughts inside you about the outcome of your plan, whatever it is. Think of the influences throughout your life from which you derived your ideas about professional achievement, money and your capabilities — and ask yourself if those ideas align with the outcome of your plan. Remember, it is you who gets to be the Architect and eventually the Commander of your mind and all its thoughts. Accepting this position allows you to choose the beliefs that support the execution of your plan or plans.

As you examine the outcome of your plan in depth, and should you discover any anchors of your own, remember what you learned in Chapter Two about eliminating any Career Inhibiting Beliefs. The exercise given in that chapter is very effective. Remember, you choose what you believe. Make your beliefs good ones. Do not allow average logic and other people's ideas of realism to define them for you. Walk out under the night sky and look upward to gain the vision of limitless possibility. Realize there are no boundaries to your ability or capability. Accept this truth as you become the Architect of your new beliefs.

Synchronizing these new beliefs throughout your entire mind allows the powerful energy within you to kick into high gear and perform the accurate, intelligent actions that contain the necessary potency to get you what you want.

Element #5:
Use Persistence to Carry Out Your Plan Over an Extended Length of Time.

In the successful pursuit of a higher aim, the man or woman who embraces persistence will always win, regardless of how many times that person is knocked down in the dirt. The importance of persistence to human achievement is simply unparalleled. No other personal trait or quality, no amount of education or financial wealth can match the raw power of persistence. Persistence is your best friend. It is your action producer when the going is at its hardest, and it will liberate you from the shackles of impossibility. The power of persistence itself is based purely on the strength of your motive. Persistence is an *attainable* character trait! It is available to any human being on the planet who has intense desire and passionate dedication to purpose.

Persistence has two distinct halves that must be fused together in order to work properly for you.

The first half of persistence: the physical habit. This is your willpower to persist despite confrontations, obstacles or barriers that attempt to stop you. The first half is fed by the never-ending fire of your concrete motive. This basic instinct of persistence engages its role as your secret weapon at a time when your plan, as well as your enthusiasm, becomes shrouded underneath a thick fog of hopelessness. It is at this crucial point that the majority of people throw up their hands and say, "I quit!", destroying all hopes of ever seeing the physical realization of their idea. How many people do you know personally that have accepted the circumstances life has handed them, without ever putting up a fight?

Not you. Not anymore. To permanently separate yourself from the masses of people who have severed themselves from their dreams by giving up, invoke the power of persistence when you feel most like abandoning your pursuit. Crank up your enthusiasm. Imagine how great it will be when you have made it to where you want to be instead of entertaining thoughts of giving up. Switch your thought track. Use control over your thoughts to give yourself that boost of "nitrous-enthusiasm" when you need it most, and move quickly out of the fog toward the finish line.

The second half of persistence: intelligent action. How exactly do you persist? You move forward and use persistence as though you are opening a combination lock that stands between you and stacks of crisp one hundred dollar bills inside a big steel safe. You don't open a safe by trying the same combination over and over again; the lock will never budge even though you are showing the first element of persistence. You will open the safe by repeatedly attempting different patterns of numbers again and again until you select the correct sequence. The safe door clicks, swings open and piles of money fall into your lap.

In my mind, the master of this method is Thomas A. Edison, who tried over ten thousand different approaches in his effort to create an electric light bulb before he found the right combination of variables that produced exactly what he had envisioned. Edison effectively harnessed both halves of persistence, and that is why he was so successful, particularly with his incandescent lamp.

Edison's illuminating invention is tangible evidence of the amazing reward for using persistence.

The key in this is to be relentless in your persistence to achieve your goals, keeping at it, for as long it takes. I have adopted a famous quote from Winston Churchill. This quote is part of who I am, and it has become the foundation for all of my other beliefs. It says,

"Never, never, never, never give up. Never give up."

Element #6:
Lock in on What You Can Do and Ignore the Rest

The completion of your plan becomes possible through keeping your mind locked in on what you are able to accomplish in the present. Focus on the elements of your plan that you can directly influence now, at this very moment. Put your effort into doing what you can, now, to move forward with your plan, using all of the resources that are readily available. Rid your mind of the negative thought processes by adopting the proper perspective on any problems that do exist. It is perfectly okay to find potential pitfalls in your plan; in fact it is good to do so. Just remember, when you do encounter a difficulties or pitfalls, see them for what they really are — <u>temporary obstacles that will be overcome!</u> How you personally view adversity will be the deciding factor in determining the success of your plan. *Remember the Great Secret!*

When you are no longer worrying about uncertainties, the door to the imagination swings wide-open. It is at this point where powerful creative energy flows in and fills your mind. This is when the answers come. Locking in on the positive aspects of your own plan is empowering, and it will allow you to get inside places that other people cannot. Never forget that you command your mind to make it do what you want. Make the decision to become aware of the polarity of your thinking processes. Are your thoughts negative or positive?

Practice locking your thoughts onto the positive and onto *what you can do*. Train yourself to look for answers rather than excuses. Using your mind in this way separates you from the millions of people whose plans have failed, people who have a never-ending list of excuses for all the things they were not able to do.

Being solution-oriented has its own benefits. The only personal risk to you for adopting this element of Science of a Successful Plan is that people might refer to you as "having a one-track mind." Concentration on the immediate action you can take to advance your plan will eliminate procrastination. Taking control of the natural processes that are at work in your mind and using that control to create an immediate action will permit you to succeed where other fail. That is my personal promise to you.

Element #7:
Cooperation From Other People will make your plan soar.

Cooperation is pure magnificence. Cooperation makes the impossible possible. There is an unmistakable power when individuals align themselves behind a single purpose. The birth of the United States of America is a brilliant example supporting this truth. Cooperation facilitates solution. Two or more minds working toward a common aspiration create a synergistic capacity. Cooperation is harnessing the power of a group and directing that power toward definite goals and exponential achievement.

There are two challenges that must be confronted for you to be successful in using cooperation. The first challenge is actually gaining the cooperation you need. The second is keeping that cooperation intact and active. The first challenge occurs when we are attempting to sell ourselves, or our ideas, to a potential partner whose help is essential to the completion of the plan. The presentation of your idea will be successful when your potential partner is able to clearly see how he will benefit.

What do you bring to the table?

Let's take a peek at value. When you are selling yourself, remember to think about the person on the other side of the desk and what their needs are. Here are some things to keep in mind. What will they receive by offering their help to you? How are you going to use their own needs to appeal to them? How are you going to help the other person attain their goals? It makes no difference whether you are approaching an individual or a company; the rules are the same. You must sell them on the opportunities you can offer. Envision how the outcome of your plan aligns with the prospect's personal goals, find the common threads and tie them together. Answer these questions before you present your plans and ideas to others for their help. Anticipate any concerns in advance. Be forthcoming with your real intentions in your approach and show how the value of your idea benefits everyone involved.

Keeping it moving.

Harmony is the key. Any type of cooperative work between people must have the element of harmony; otherwise the entire effort will sink like a stone. With the inherent diversity that is present in all living people, maintaining harmony can often be difficult. The cultivation and use of harmony between people is possible through using temperance of ego. It is possible through active listening. It is possible through keeping your mind open. Harmony must flow back and forth between all members of a cooperative alliance, and if harmony begins to fade, it can be revived through an enthusiastic injection of the initial motives that formed the cooperative alliance. Chapter Five in this book, "The Most Valuable Skill" gives you some effective tools and ideas for building and maintaining the bridge of cooperation.

Element #8:
Your winning tactic: Consistent, Focused Action

Ideas, knowledge, plans and information all are completely useless without the magic, life-giving ingredient of action. So many people are looking for the quick fix, the instant solution for getting exactly what they want right now. The truth is that big results and significant changes come through small, repetitive actions that are focused on a definite purpose over a period of time. Examples of this can be seen everywhere. Look at every successful business that has ever been built, at every good book that has ever been written and at every blockbuster movie that has ever been made. None of them were started and then completed in the same day. They were all constructed through the combination of smaller, repetitive actions that built onto one another to eventually yield the specific outcome.

There is only one thing that can possibly hold you back, and that is a nasty little thing called procrastination. Procrastination is the insidious enemy of action. If permitted, procrastination can take your plan and destroy it one piece at a time, secretly and silently. Procrastination seems harmless and it is an easy tendency to develop. Fighting this deadly enemy is a perpetual battle that must be won on a daily basis. Action is a habit. Just like any other habit, it can be developed to the point that action is engaged automatically by recognizing procrastination and choosing the opposite course.

To be brutally effective, the action habit must be enforced over an extended period of time. The other elements in this chapter are designed to help you answer the "call to action". Motive, Vision, Confidence, Synchronicity, Persistence, Concentration and Cooperation all support this primary canon action. Action is what gets things done. Action drives you to the realization of your dream. This may seem overly simple or somewhat superfluous, but, believe me, this tiny little fact eludes millions. Do not be one of them. Instead, do something *everyday* towards the attainment of your plan. It does not matter the size of the action, just that action is taken. Demand this of yourself!

Remember to Relax and Have Fun

Working for the achievement of something is a very empowering and wonderful thing. The only thing that is greater is spending time with the people in your life who you love and care for. Remember to balance your efforts with good old-fashioned relaxation. Take time for yourself once in a while. Slow down and stay in harmony with your family and environment. Play with your children. Laugh out loud. Do something romantic for your spouse. Grab cold lemonade and go sit in the shade for a few hours. Sleep in once and while; you'll feel better. This very important piece of information was missing from every success philosophy that I studied. It is absolutely necessary. Relaxation and leisure allows you to consider how precious and wonderful your life is.

SUMMARY:
Elements of the Science of a Successful Plan

Element #1 Create Your Powerful Vision.

Element #2 Build a Concrete Motive.

Element #3 Believe in Yourself .

Element #4 Synchronize your plan's ultimate outcome between both halves of your mind.

Element #5 Use Persistence to carry out your plan over an extended period of time.

Element #6 Lock in on what you Can Do and Forget the Rest.

Element #7 Cooperation from other People will make your Plan Soar.

Element #8 Your Winning Tactic: Consistent, Focused Action

Lastly – HAVE FUN

A Final Word...

The realization of my own dreams will come true only if this book has made a positive impact in your life. My purpose in sharing this philosophy with you is to bring forth the powerful forces that exist inside you - help you harness and direct those forces toward definite ends. You have the capability to transform your deepest desires into a living reality. This is the universal truth of the infinite power of your being.

In closing, I want to express my sincere gratitude to you for sharing your time with me in this book.

Thank you!

"Do not go where the path may lead, go instead where there is no path and leave a trail."
-Ralph Waldo Emerson

About the Author

Employed as a Telecommunications Engineer for the last decade, Chris Henson was faced with ultimate adversity in 2001 when America's economy received a devastating blow. The technology sector, without a doubt, took the force of the collapse, loosing over 500,000 high-skilled professionals to layoffs in just a four month period. To meet this challenge head-on and avoid the coming tsunami of layoff rounds, Chris relentlessly pursued the Science of Achievement from every possible angle.

Transforming the knowledge into action, Chris managed to do what millions of people could not do; keep his job. Not only did Chris keep his job and avoid multiple waves of layoff rounds, he charged ahead, attaining new positions with higher pay during the worst technology recession in history.

Chris is a Father of two wonderful sons, Jacob and Casey. Happily married to his wife Vanessa, Chris and his family enjoy living in the beautiful city of Broomfield, Colorado. Chris has obtained four nationally recognized career certifications from Cisco Systems; as well as two specialized certifications from the Computing Technology Industry Association. As an active member in the High Tech Industry, Chris works for a multi-million dollar e-commerce office supply company in Broomfield, Colorado, supporting critical Data and Telecommunications Networks. Chris also holds Certificates for Excelled Speech, Certified NTAC Instructor, and also highly enjoys motivational speaking.

www.ingramcontent.com/pod-product-compliance
Lightning Source LLC
Chambersburg PA
CBHW032004170526
45157CB00002B/543